Building Community Strengths

Community Development Foundation

The Community Development Foundation (CDF) was set up in 1968 to pioneer new forms of community development.

CDF strengthens communities by ensuring the effective participation of people in determining the conditions which affect their lives. It does this through:

- providing support for community initiatives
- promoting best practice
- informing policy-makers at local and national level.

As a leading authority on community development in the UK and Europe, CDF is a non-departmental public body and is supported by the Voluntary and Community Division of the Department of National Heritage. It receives substantial backing from local and central government, trusts and business.

CDF promotes community development through:

- local action projects
- conferences and seminars
- consultancies and training programmes
- research and evaluation services
- parliamentary and public policy analysis
- information services
- *CDF News*
- publications.

Chairman: Sir Alan Haselhurst, MP
Chief Executive: Alison West

Community Development Foundation
60 Highbury Grove
London N5 2AG

Tel: 0171 226 5375
Fax: 0171 704 0313
Email: 106043.1620@compuserve.com
http://www.vois.org.uk/CDF

Registered Charity Number: 306130

Building Community Strengths

A Resource Book on Capacity Building

By Steve Skinner

Supported by John Laing plc

COMMUNITY DEVELOPMENT FOUNDATION
• PUBLICATIONS •

First published in Great Britain in 1997 by
Community Development Foundation
60 Highbury Grove
London N5 2AG

Reprinted 1997, 1998

Cover design and typesetting by The Bears Communications, Amsterdam

Printed in Great Britain by Crowes of Norwich

British Library Cataloguing-in-Publication data

A record of this publication is available from the British Library

ISBN 0902406 78 7

In memory of Rooney Martin

I'm not just a service user...

No I'm not just a service user,
I'm not just a face in the queue,
I'm not just a mum or a member,
I'm a person through and through.

I'm not just the blind or the needy,
Not just one of the deserving few,
So don't give me your charity handouts,
I'm a person through and through.

And I'm not just a wheelchair user,
That others so often see through,
And I'm not just the homeless in doorways,
I'm a person through and through.

I'm not just your client or helper,
Not a vandal or sniffer of glue,
And I'm not the grassroots or just local,
I'm a person through and through.

And I'm not just a single parent,
And my kids aren't a problem to you,
And I'm not just the gypsy they're moving again,
I'm a person through and through.

So I'm not just a service user,
I'm not just a face in the queue,
I'm not just a name or a number,
I'm a person through and through.

So it's time now to drop all your labels,
Start talking both straight and true,
Cos I'm me with my rights, my loves and my fights,
Watch out now cos I'm coming through,
Watch out now cos I'm coming through.

Steve Skinner

Contents

Credits and thanks

CDF wishes to fully acknowledge the contributions made to the production of this resource book by a wide range of projects, agencies and practitioners. In particular we wish to thank the following people for their useful comments on the text:

Mandy Wilson, Standing Conference for Community Development; Val Harris, Val Harris Training; John Mathews, BASSAC; Keith Nathan, Leeds Voluntary Sector Network; Jan Smithies and Georgina Webster, Labyrinth Training and Consultancy; Inge Shepherd; Rosemary Gray, Steve Boyle, Batley City Challenge; Murray Hawtin, Leeds Metropolitan University; Audrey Bronstein, Oxfam; Caroline Knighton and Simon Robinson, Business in the Community; Ebrahim Dockrat, Calderdale and Kirklees TEC; Peter Berkowitz, European Commission DGXVI; David Wilcox, Partnership; Steve Trimmins, Home Office Adviser, Yorkshire and Humberside Government Office.

CDF would like to thank The Industrial Society and acknowledge its contribution to CDF's work on capacity building.

CDF would especially like to thank John Laing plc for its financial contribution towards the costs of this publication.

Introduction

Thanks are due to the following for providing ideas and information: Steve Trimmins, Home Office Advisor, Yorkshire and Humberside Government Office; Peter Berkowitz, European Commission DGXVI; John Armstrong, June Lightfoot, and Peter Dale.

Part 1

Thanks for ideas and information from the People's Group, and the Canterbury Partnership Trust, Bradford.

Part 2

• *Action-based learning and Qualifications and accreditation:*
  the text for these sections was kindly written by Pete Wilde of the Federation of Community Work Training Groups.

Thanks are due to the following for providing information and ideas:

• *Consortium-based learning:*
  Marlene McEachrance and Sarah Lee from Capacity Unlimited.

• *Community mentoring:*
  Angela Lewis-Wright from East London Community Training; the Belle Isle Foundation, Leeds; the Royds Community Association, Bradford.

• *Secondments:*
  Yorkshire and Humberside BitC for helpful comments and information.

- *Capacity building with refugees:*
  Refugee Action.

- MaTReC case study:
  Neil Coulson.

- *The Hackney standard:*
  The Civic Trust.

- *The Management NVQ:*
  York CVS.

- *Batley case study:*
  Batley Action.

- *The organisational health check:*
  Val Harris and Nottingham CVS.

- *The training needs survey form was based on an original developed by:*
  the Voluntary Sector Training Unit, TAD Centre, Middlesbrough, with additions from the form used for Batley City Challenge.

Thanks are due to Roger Walker, Leeds Social Services for helpful comments on organisational training needs and to Oxfam for information on development projects in the Lebanon and East Africa.

Part 3

- *The Bradford City Challenge Case Study:*
  Most of the fieldwork for this consultancy was carried out by John Harris of John Harris Training and Consultancy.

- *For ideas, information and comments, thanks are also due to:*
  Bethnal Green City Challenge, Bradford City Challenge; John Harris; Jenny Hyatt and Roger Walker.

Part 4

- *The concept of community infrastructure*
  was given to the author by Labyrinth Training and Consultancy.

- *For information on resource centres:*
  Brigid Kane, Head of Community Resources, Barnsley Metropolitan Borough Council..

- *For ideas on the role of networks:*
  SCCD.

- *For use of the draft definition of community work:*
  the England Interim Board for Community Work Training and Qualifications.

- *Case study on the Pan-London Capacity Building Programme* based on information provided by John Mathews, BASSAC and June Lightfoot.

- *For comments on resources:*
  Inge Shepherd.

- *For comments on the text on community work:*
  Pete Wilde, Federation of Community Work Training Groups.

- *For the text on resources and the private sector:*
  Business in the Community, Yorkshire and Humberside.

- *For information on the Professional Firms Group:*
  Business in the Community.

- *For information on the Organisation Check for Partnerships:*
  Val Harris.

- *For information on links with community enterprises:*
  The Body Shop International.

- *The Netherton case study:*
  The Netherton Partnership Board.

Part 5

- *Thanks for information from:*
  Chris Purnell, Community Support Commissioning, Brent Borough Council; Steve Boyle, Batley City Challenge Action; Alison Dickens, Bethnal Green City Challenge; Graham Duncan, Hackney Task Force; Melanie Griffin and Dave Hague, The European Secretariat, Yorkshire and Humberside; Kevin Hopkins, Yorkshire and Humberside Government Office.

Introduction

Capacity building is a systematic approach to assisting community organisations to play a major part in the regeneration of their neighbourhoods. Increasingly community organisations are becoming involved in local partnerships, in the management of projects and services and in the creation of community enterprise. They have a wealth of expertise and experience to contribute but are also actively requesting help with training, organisational development and resources to enable them to have a full and lasting impact on neighbourhood regeneration.

This publication is a resource book on capacity building, describing a variety of approaches and proposing a framework for longer term area based strategies. It includes case studies, checklists and practical guidelines, drawing on the experience, skills and ideas of a wide range of projects and programmes.

It has been written for:

- practitioners who are directly working with community organisations – community development workers, trainers, project organisers, advisers and voluntary sector support staff

- policy makers and managers who are involved in funding and implementing regeneration programmes – based in local authorities, government offices for the regions, central government departments, funding organisations, regeneration agencies, TECs, and the private sector.

The aims of this publication are:

- to increase understanding of the nature and potential of capacity building

- to enable practitioners to work with community organisations to make capacity building wider in scope and to produce capacity building plans

- to enable policy makers and managers to more effectively fund and organise capacity building programmes and to devise area based strategies for capacity building.

In the community sector there is already a wealth of ideas, skills, knowledge and abilities.

Capacity building has great potential to strengthen the ability of community organisations to achieve their aims. In the community sector there is already a wealth of ideas, skills, knowledge and abilities, often unrecognised or underestimated by outside agencies and organisations. The approach to capacity building described in this resource book is firmly based on a recognition of this wealth and aims to build on existing strengths and experience.

A definition of capacity building

The definition of capacity building we are using for this publication is:

Development work that strengthens the ability of community organisations and groups to build their structures, systems, people and skills so that they are better able to define and achieve their objectives and engage in consultation and planning, manage community projects and take part in partnerships and community enterprises.

It includes aspects of training, organisational and personal development and resource building, organised in a planned and self-conscious manner, reflecting the principles of empowerment and equality.

Many voluntary agencies, local authorities, consultants, trainers and community development workers – paid and unpaid – have for a number of years already been involved in the process of building skills and developing grassroots community organisations.

What's specific about capacity building?
- It's systematic – it involves taking a full and detailed look at training and organisational development needs
- It's comprehensive – it involves looking at the needs of individuals in the community organisation, the organisation itself as well as the environment in which the organisation operates
- It's forward looking – as well as taking stock of the existing situation, it's a way of helping community groups to plan ahead in terms of the skills and type of organisation needed to achieve future aims.

Fundamentally, capacity building is not a new approach to working with community organisations in its own right; however these three features in combination help to identify it. In this resource book we use the term capacity building to refer to development work that is:
- primarily concerned with the activities of groups and community organisations, rather than focusing on the individual's own needs *per se*. A useful distinction can be made here between individual capacity building, a term often associated with vocational training, and community capacity building which is the concern of this publication, as reflected in the definition given above
- primarily concerned with community groups and the community sector, rather than professional voluntary organisations. Obviously many of the points and approaches described will be of relevance to professional voluntary sector organisations.

Even within this more specific definition of capacity building, the areas of skill, knowledge and ability are very varied, depending on the aims and activities of the community group. Some of the particular issues for community enterprises, for example, are explored in the text, though overall our approach in this publication to draw out common themes for community based groups and organisations, leaving readers to adapt and adopt this material to the needs of the particular groups they are working with.

Questions and answers about capacity building
Here are common all questions often asked by practitioners, members of community groups and managers of regeneration programmes.

Where does the term capacity building come from?

As a term capacity building was used widely in the United States associated with the introduction of legislation called the Community Investment Act. This promoted community based investment schemes with associated capacity building programmes with a focus on business skills and economic development. This emphasis on capacity building mainly in relation to community economic development is in contrast to the wider definition given to it in this publication.

As a term isn't it rather patronising towards members of community groups?

Yes, it is. However, it is the term now being used widely by local authorities, government departments and regeneration agencies, so the issue is how to ensure it is at least interpreted and used in a way that reflects community development principles. We argue the starting point of any capacity programme should be to recognise and appreciate the wealth of existing skills, experience, vision and talent in the community sector. We also promote the need for professional capacity building to run in parallel to community based capacity building. Staff and managers in public organisations active in regeneration areas themselves often need to increase their understanding of the community and voluntary sector and their ability to communicate and work effectively with community representatives.

Haven't we already been doing this for years?

Many community development workers and other community practitioners have for many years been involved in facilitating individual learning and organisational change in their work with community organisations. We argue, as discussed earlier, that capacity building has three features that in combination give it a distinct and definable role within community development. Capacity building as a particular approach also makes use of methods that may be new to some community development workers, such as training needs analysis and techniques involved in organisational development. These are described in Parts 2 and 3.

Isn't capacity building just another term for community development support?

In Part 4 we examine the role and meaning of community development support for community organisations, focusing on the skills and approaches involved in community work. We argue that there is a difference and in particular that capacity building should only ever be additional to – rather than a substitute for – well resourced community development support.

Isn't this just a diversion from the real issue of proper levels of resources for community organisations?

As an approach to community development, capacity building could be interpreted to wrongly imply that the main block to groups being effective is a lack of skills and structures. In contrast, we argue capacity building needs to be additional resources rather than a substitute for a proper level of ongoing mainstream provision. In particular, as discussed in Part 4, to be effective it needs to be complementary to – rather than replacing – community development support. In the longer run, capacity building itself will help to build the ability of groups to obtain proper levels of ongoing mainstream funding.

Doesn't capacity building lead to a loss of key community leaders as they gain in skills and move from the area?

A fear expressed by some regeneration agencies is that having invested in the training of community leaders, these individuals then move to new areas. However, in practice this occurs in only a small number of cases. The impact of such a loss to the regeneration area can be reduced by adopting a more broad-based capacity building programme, focusing more on groups and less on individual leaders.

Isn't capacity building mainly about increasing access to vocational training?

Based on the definition given earlier, the aim of capacity building is to primarily increase the effectiveness of community organisations. This process will obviously have secondary benefits of increasing the levels of skills and employability of individuals, as discussed further in Part 2.

So, is capacity building just about developing new skills in community groups?

No, to begin with, for the individual, it can be about far more than just skills – it also includes using people's talents, building on their experience and strengthening their confidence. In addition, to be effective, capacity building needs to be more than a process of enhancing skills and developing community structures; it is also about communities having an ability to influence and a direct impact on decisions directly affecting them.

But will funders and regeneration agencies be interested in funding capacity building provision?

There are increasing opportunities in current funding programmes for capacity building activities to be funded. In the SRB Challenge Fund, for example, the Bidding Guidance for Round Three stated that it supports initiatives that among other objectives will enhance the quality of life and capacity to contribute to local regeneration of local people: 'Capacity building activities can be funded where that capacity building contributes to an overall, comprehensive regeneration strategy' (Home Office Adviser, May 1996).

Equally, in the case of the European Structural Funds: 'Within almost all parts of Objective One, Two and Five B Programmes and the RECHAR and URBAN Community Initiatives, capacity building can be supported in the context of community economic development,' (DG16 Official, European Commission, May 1996 (see case study in Part 5)).

The structure of this book

This book is divided into five main parts:

Part 1: Introduction to Capacity Building

Part 1 explores capacity building in the light of three themes identified as central to the context of regeneration in the late 1990s. These three themes are partnerships, sustainability and equal opportunities. Part 1 is completed with a case study, and we draw out principles that can contribute towards a basis for the provision of capacity building.

Part 2: Developing People

Part 2 describes a variety of forms of training, including group and course-based training, community mentoring, secondments, placements, visits and consortium-based learning. It explores increased employability associated with capacity building and then examines training in the light of two themes of empowerment and equality. Part 2 finishes with practical guidelines on identifying training needs and a set of policy recommendations for the resourcing of effective training.

Part 3: Developing Organisations

Part 3 gives a general introduction to the practice of organisational development and in particular explores roles that outside specialists can take. It offers a set of practical guidelines on how to make the best use of specialist help. Part 3 includes a set of policy recommendations for the resourcing of organisational development.

Part 4: Developing Community Infrastructure

The community infrastructure is part of the environment within which community organisations operate. This includes resources, networking, participation structures, community development support and professional capacity building. Part 4 examines these five forms and includes a number of policy recommendations for agencies wishing to further develop community infrastructure.

Part 5: Developing Plans and Strategies

Part 5 examines options for devising and implementing an area-based strategy for capacity building, in particular using a framework of five key roles for the community in regeneration. It also describes how to devise and prepare a capacity building plan with community organisations and introduces the issues involved in the evaluation of capacity building.

How to use this book

This publication is a practical resource book, and includes:

- *Examples and short case studies to highlight points in the text.* In many cases we include contact telephone numbers of the organisations the information originates from. You can contact them for more information if needed but please use this opportunity with discretion.

- *Information on relevant publications.* These are listed at the end of each section and are an important complement to the main text, which often has the role of introducing a particular issue or theme rather than covering it in any great depth.
- *Checklists and practical guidelines.* These are intended primarily for practitioners involved in direct work with community organisations. The points they contain obviously need to be adapted to the needs of the particular group with which you are working.
- *Policy recommendations.* These are placed at various points in the publication and are intended for use at policy level by regeneration agencies and funders.

Because this publication is targeted at a variety of audiences – practitioners, managers and policy makers – it is expected that any one reader will focus on those sections of most relevance to them.

While in places we offer recommendations, it is essential that capacity building is approached with flexibility and sensitivity to the needs of the organisation and the area. Although this publication focuses on regeneration in urban settings, much of the information and ideas will also be useful when adapted to the specific needs of rural and semi-rural areas, especially where the latter are former coalfield communities.

Terms used

Community group: We use this term to mean local community groups or community organisations which include a substantial element of activity and control by local residents in a voluntary capacity. These groups may be active because of a shared location – such as a tenant association – or because of a shared identity or shared interests, such as a disability group. These groups may or may not have some paid staff and be formally constituted for example as a charity or a company limited by guarantee. They do not include organisations consisting primarily of paid staff using volunteer help.

Voluntary sector organisations: Groups whose activities are carried out other than for profit but which are not public or local authorities. These organisations would normally be formally constituted and employ paid professional and administrative staff. They may or may not use volunteer help.

The community sector: The whole range of autonomous collective activity, directly undertaken by individuals within their neighbourhood or community of interest, to improve collective life and conditions. It is a spectrum which extends from the community groups and similar informal activities as a whole in one area.

Regeneration agency: We use the term 'regeneration agency' to refer to partnerships funded by, for example, the Single Regeneration Budget Challenge Fund and/or European Structural Funds, City Challenge companies, Task Forces and similar agencies directly involved in develo-

ping and managing an area-based development programme on a time limited basis.

Task Forces: The Task Forces, which started in 1986, were area-based, inter-departmental government regeneration agencies. The main emphasis of their work was on training and creating job opportunities. In 1992/3, the Task Force programme was amalgamated into the Single Regeneration Budget. Since then, existing Task Forces have been closing as they reach the end of their normal five-year working life.

Practitioner: By this we mean community workers, trainers, training organisers, group workers, community consultants, experienced community activists, and a wide range of people involved in community development as a part of their work activities.

The material in this book is based on:

- discussions and interviews with practitioners, managers and policy makers in a wide range of regeneration agencies, community projects and training organisations

- CDF's own field work experience and theoretical contribution to capacity building and regeneration. In particular the work of the Canterbury Partnership Trust in Bradford – where CDF has had substantial community work involvement – forms a major case study at various points in this publication

- a major conference on Capacity Building with Black and Minority Ethnic Groups, held at Ruskin College in Oxford in September 1995, arranged jointly by the Standing Conference for Community Development and CDF. This event brought together a large number of white, black and minority ethnic activists, practitioners, managers and policy makers from regeneration agencies, the voluntary sector and community organisations.

All quotes in the text are real although since contributors wanted to remain anonymous, only the background of the person is given, rather than their name. Many quotes are from the Oxford Conference on Capacity Building with Black and Minority Ethnic Groups. These are referred to as originating from 'The Oxford Conference'.

We now set the scene for regeneration in the late 1990s and the implications for capacity building.

Part 1
Introduction to Capacity Building

Capacity building and regeneration

Capacity building is a use-ful concept that may help to bring new resources to community sector organisations.

There are many changes happening in the context of community development and regeneration in Britain in the late 1990s. We believe that especially during this period of change, capacity building is a useful concept that may help to bring new resources to community sector organisations and increase the effectiveness of regeneration programmes.

The aim of Part 1 is to explore capacity building in the light of three themes related to context of regeneration. These themes are:

• partnerships,

• sustainability and

• equal opportunities.

Part 1 ends with a case study, exploring the role of capacity building in estate-based regeneration.

Partnerships

This term is now being applied to a whole host of initiatives and relationships, often undeservedly. Partnerships can take a variety of forms, and it's useful to be aware of this variety. Here are three examples:

• at district level, a local authority, in developing bids of various rounds of the Single Regeneration Budget Challenge Fund, forms a partnership with the Chamber of Commerce, the Training and Enterprise Council (TEC), a university and city-wide representatives of the voluntary and community sector.

• at area level, associated with one round of SRB Challenge Funds, an area-based partnership is established with representatives of the local authority, the TEC, doorstep companies and local voluntary and community organisations.

• at neighbourhood level, a community association establishes itself as a registered charity and invites representatives of the police, local businesses and the local mosque onto its board of trustees.

Partnerships vary tremendously in the power balance between partners and their level of meaningful involvement for community organisations. In extreme cases, some community organisations found themselves described as 'partners' in SRB Challenge Fund bids when the local authority made no contact with them at all about the bid's content! Certainly the term partnership has now become fashionable and respectable, though the motives of some partners may often be mixed, driven by opportunism

rather than any real commitment to community involvement. For example, a survey of SRB Challenge Fund bids for 1995 found:

'Most lead partners, TECs and local authorities have been driven by the desire to replace lost or unreliable funding. This has often led to the submission of already well worked up projects excluding the possibility of real partnership with the voluntary and community sector on developing these schemes' (Clarke 1995).

A sample of successful Round Two bids revealed that 37% of respondents regarded the community sector as marginal or not important.

A further random survey representing 12 per cent of all successful Round Two bids, suggests that partnerships can be divided into four types according to the level of involvement of their members. Within a continuum between 'shell' and 'autonomous' partnerships, the survey revealed in the majority of bids that partnership working fell short of even adequate participation levels. In particular, many community and voluntary organisations felt excluded and were not involved until late in the bidding process. In terms of which sectors led bids in Round Two, according to the DoE database, there were only eight community-led bids and six voluntary sector-led bids. These sectors also experienced a reduction in the allocation of Challenge Fund resources from 3.1 per cent of Round One total lifetime allocations to 1.65 per cent in Round Three (Hall et al, 1996).

These moves reflect the growth in numbers of community based partnerships, a trend that is likely to continue.

Some key points about partnerships are:

'Our own representative on the SRB Board until recently had an annual budget of only £275 a year to 'consult the community'!
An SRB Partnership

- There is the question as to what extent partnerships are in reality, based on equal relationships. When community organisations have partners who are large scale funders of regeneration initiatives in their area, their experience may be quite different. In such situations – which are the rule rather than the exception – it is more effective to acknowledge the difference of power in the relationship. The nature of the relationship can become a negotiated and explicit agreement rather than a blurring of the issues under the vague banner of 'equality' between players. Bear in mind also that community representatives themselves may often represent different and even conflicting interests within the 'community'

- While the relationship may not be equal in terms of financial resources, it is important to remember community organisations may have other resources to offer partnerships – organisational skills, local knowledge, neighbourhood contacts, network relationships, a large membership for consultations, energy, time and above all, commitment.

'We want you to listen, to get to know us.'
Community leader

Community-based partnerships offer regeneration agencies an increased chance to continue the initiative beyond the agencies' own life span, increased opportunities for co-ordination at neighbourhood level and a degree of 'street credibility'. Community involvement is also increasingly required as part of government-funded regeneration programmes such as SRB Challenge Fund and some European Structural Funds programmes. Because of this variety of benefits for the regeneration agency, it is important for community organisations entering partnerships with them to remember the significance of their contribution. Armed with such growing recognition of the value of their role, many community organisations involved in partnerships are now more assertively pointing out their rights and expectations.

The implications of these points for capacity building are:

- *Recognising the pressures.* Regeneration agencies need to recognise the pressures being placed on community organisations through their participation in partnerships. Volunteer members of groups, now put forward as representatives and delegates of their organisation or neighbourhood, are in effect required to have a sophisticated level of management and communication skills. Participation in partnerships consequently needs resource provision to assist the growth of skill and confidence of community representatives. This need is being recognised officially in some quarters. For example, the Strategic Development Scheme in Wales – the Welsh equivalent of the SRB – in 1995 recognised the value of strong community sector structures and set the building up of these as hard targets in the programmes (Welsh Office 1995)

- *Two sides of the coin.* Equally the need for capacity building should not be seen as only existing in the community sector. Many professional workers from regeneration agencies now involved in partnerships have a low level of development of their own communication skills for engaging with groups or understanding the issues of community development. Capacity building needs to be equally explored with agency staff involved in community initiatives and partnerships. In this sense capacity building, in the context of community development, is a dualistic approach. This point is returned to and explored further in Part 4.

As you can see, the increasing interest in partnerships is creating new needs for capacity building.

Sustainability

Sustainability has now become a prime concern of regeneration agencies in Britain in the 1990s. What do we mean by sustainability? Some useful questions that help to define sustainability are:

- Have individual community projects achieved lasting benefits?

- Has the overall initiative tackled the underlying cause of the problem?

- Has there been a wider impact on the long-term behaviour of other service providers in the area? (DoE 1992)

- Are there local structures in place that continue to thrive and contribute to the regeneration of the area after the completion of the life-span of the regeneration agency?

In this context the term sustainability does not primarily refer to environmental sustainability.

Overall, sustainability has become a concern at three levels:

- *at community level,* as groups and organisations have become suspicious of short term, top down interventions that after completion can leave them with many of the same problems as before

- *at agency level,* especially those such as City Challenge and Housing Action Trusts who now have only two or three years left. While City Challenge partnerships were meant to consider sustainability from the start of their programme activities, for some this has only recently become a priority

- *at government level,* as there is growing evidence available of the limited lasting impact of programmes and the repeated need for resource allocation to depressed urban areas. It is now firmly established that SRB Challenge Fund resourced regeneration programmes include provision for both completion and succession (Clarke 1995).

However despite this interest in and concern about sustainability, a comprehensive study of a variety of regeneration programmes in depressed urban areas, including City Challenge and Task Forces, shows them to date as limited in their ability to stimulate such lasting impact (Fordham 1995). The programmes, which have historically been time limited and area based have suffered from a variety of problems that have reduced their sustainability. In some cases there was an inadequate analysis of the cause of the deprivation in the target area; in others, the action programmes that were developed did not always focus on the acknowledged cause! Research by the Department of the Environment's own Inner Cities Research Programme, reviewing urban programmes of the last ten years, concluded that:

'The emphasis on infrastructure in the programmes of urban regeneration has ignored the needs of deprived inner-area residents and has missed the opportunity to utilise their skills and to mobilise their support' (DoE 1994).

The indications are that a planned approach to sustainability requires capacity building to be integrated into regeneration programmes from the beginning. But beware – there are still a variety of views of the term sustainability. Approaches that see it as primarily a financial arrangement – just securing new sources of funding as existing ones taper down – are still a long way from appreciating the role of community participation and empowerment. In contrast, other approaches aim to establish ongoing community based structures that have their continuity enhanced through a transfer of assets during the lifetime of the regeneration programme.

The implications of these points for capacity building are:

- *Capacity building is becoming an essential element of effective sustainability.* Recent research funded by the Joseph Rowntree Foundation suggests local empowerment and capacity building is perhaps the key issue in promoting sustainability. Other factors include programme design, project management and the composition of continuation strategies (DoE 1994).

- *If the community sector and its effective participation is increasingly seen as a key building block to programme implementation, this supports the case for properly-funded capacity building provision.* In other words, the evidence suggests capacity building is not an optional extra to urban regeneration but an essential component and should be resourced on this basis.

- *Given this significance, it also suggests that a strategy for capacity building is needed within each regeneration programme area.* This could be a policy that involves the development of skills, organisations and resources; these ideas are developed in Parts 2, 3 and 4 of this publication. The role of area based strategies for capacity building is explored further in Part 5.

Equal opportunities

'We need to create grass-roots based movements that have a big say about how these regeneration schemes are designed in the first place.'
Community work manager

Equal opportunities as a value base in community development has rightly encouraged practitioners, in addition to focusing on neighbourhoods, to work with groups defined by identity – such as black, disability, and women's groups. This shift has also contributed to the growing importance of networking as a way of enabling joint working and campaigning between groups (Meekosha 1993). Some groups and organisations have taken on equality issues so that it underlies all areas of their work and activities. However, at individual and agency level the integration of equal opportunities into area regeneration policies and practice is still very limited:

- *At individual level,* to be effective equality principles need at least to be taken up in the hearts and minds of individuals so that there is a personal commitment to change; otherwise institutional changes are often half-measure and polices mostly remain on paper.

- *At agency level,* a key limitation is where policies are adopted the emphasis is still solely on responding to the needs of disadvantaged minorities rather than seeing equal opportunities also as a framework for initiatives that values the contribution of different groups and perspectives within an area. The former view tends to emphasise only the problems of particular communities, seeing them as minorities being excluded from the existing mainstream. In contrast, the latter view can emphasise and celebrate the cultural and social diversity of neighbourhoods as a solid platform for regeneration.

The implications of this for capacity building are:

- Bridge building between different marginalised groups, to share experiences and form campaigning networks, is essential to create grass-roots-based movements that could have a wider impact on programme planners and resource holders. Capacity building can be a part of this bridge building, by providing opportunities where experience and ideas can be shared and further skills of campaigning and networking developed.

- Equal opportunities principles affects not only the content of capacity building programmes but obviously the form it takes as well. It raises questions about venues, access, child care, publicity and so on; these are explored further in Part 2.

- One concern is the fragmentation of training and development with community organisations into separate and specific issue based areas of race, gender, disability and so on, without it being organised in a way that regularly brings exploration together. Research carried out by the West Yorkshire Racial Justice Programme, for example, shows that there has been a decline over the last few years in white trainers being involved in anti-racist training work as it is increasingly left as an area of work to black trainers.

'We need to remember the fight for equal opportunities is about challenging discrimination wherever it occurs rather than just gaining ground for our own particular cause.'
Community leader

- Capacity building in urban regeneration is a major opportunity to keep alive the importance of equal opportunities as a values base for change in cities and in communities. Given the pace of change in the voluntary and community sector and the demands of new pressures of partnership and sustainability as described earlier, there is an added need to maintain the momentum that has been built up by practitioners and campaigners over a long period of time.

Policy recommendations

Principles underlying capacity building

Capacity building needs to be organised on the basis of a clearly-defined set of principles. The following themes and points have been drawn out in Part 1 regarding these underlying principles:

- The community and voluntary sector has a wealth of skill, knowledge, awareness, energy and ideas to contribute to the regeneration of neighbourhoods and communities in Britain. Capacity building strategies and provision needs to recognise this resource and build from strengths.

- Capacity building should be organised in a way that values and appreciates cultural diversity, drawing on different cultures and traditions to contribute to best practice.

- Capacity building also needs to be organised in a way that recognises discrimination and exclusion experienced by many groups in Britain, and as a provision of resources itself helps to challenge inequalities in neighbourhoods and communities.

- The level of resource provision of capacity building as a part of regeneration needs to reflect the growing pressures experienced by community and voluntary organisations associated with the themes of partnerships and sustainability.

- Capacity building provision should be based on proper assessment of the needs of the community and voluntary sector and, where possible, groups and organisations should be supported in drawing up their own capacity building plans.

- The evidence suggests capacity building is becoming essential for the effective implementation and sustainability of regeneration programmes. Consequently, it should be properly resourced as part of the regeneration initiative and planned for from an early stage.

Discussion

The identification and use of principles in establishing plans and strategies for capacity building at both community organisation and area level is important to ensure that programmes are organised and resourced effectively. The current reality in urban regeneration initiatives in this respect is a mixed picture. Information collected for this publication revealed that while there were many examples of good practice – reflected in the case studies and examples included in the text – there were many more cases of inadequately prepared schemes, devised with little consideration of underlying principles. By not considering such issues, partnerships and organisers of capacity building schemes have been able to fall into a number of traps, for example:

- consulting only in a token manner with a limited and unrepresentative range of community organisations and often only the larger voluntary organisations

- devising schemes with little initial assessment of training and development needs

- organising provision on the assumption that capacity building is primarily a process of individual skill development rather than also addressing the need for the development of the community infrastructure.

Summary

'What is the nature of the context within which capacity building takes place? The external environment is not neutral – the main issue is not just about developing new skills. Given the context of the centralisation of power and structural social injustice, the role of communities in society needs to be examined.'
Senior manager, national voluntary organisation

Part 1 has begun to look at some of the issues for capacity building in the context of urban change in the 1990s and recognise some of the key pressures community organisations are dealing with. Capacity building cannot be organised and resourced without recognition of this wider context, which is examined more fully in publications listed below. Part One also suggests that capacity building can not be viewed as a marginal element, added on only when the main physical and economic components of the regeneration strategy are in place, but is increasingly central to achieving sustainable changes that will have lasting impact.

A wealth of skill and experience is being built up at grassroots level through the talents and energies of thousands of individuals and organisations working with energy and commitment to help to improve their own communities.

After introducing our major case study for this publication, we then move on to look at how this wealth of skill, knowledge and experience can be built on through a variety of forms of training.

Case study:
The Canterbury Partnership Trust, Bradford

This case study explores the role of capacity building in estate based regeneration. The Canterbury Partnership Trust case study is returned to at several points during this publication, to demonstrate different points about community development and capacity building.

The Canterbury estate in Bradford, only a mile from the city centre, has suffered from high levels of crime and unemployment and was once described by the local paper as 'the estate from Hell'. A survey showed that a third of adults felt unsafe walking around during the day; the area also suffered from environmental problems of neglect and a lack of play facilities. The estate of 1170 houses is mostly council-owned housing stock, which over recent years have been improved through an Estate Action Programme.

'Our vision – we are committed to improving life on the Canterbury estate through the work of the Partnership.'
The People's Group

The People's Group, a grassroots residents' association based on the Canterbury estate, has now set up an innovative Partnership Trust to bring new life to the area. The aim of the Trust is to raise funds for improvements on the estate, act as a local voice and co-ordinate new schemes and community initiatives. A key feature is that the Trust is grassroots controlled – residents have the majority of places on the board. This is in contrast to many development trusts or partnerships that are in practice dominated by the 'great and the good' – outside 'professionals' who may not represent the area. On the partnership board, ten places are for local residents from across the whole of the estate and seven places for representatives from the police, the local authority, local business and religious communities. The board is supported by a community worker employed by CDF and a partnership manager employed by the Housing Directorate.

The role of capacity building

The People's Group decided in 1995, a year before the Trust was established, that a programme of capacity building was needed to assist their members and other community leaders to build their skills and knowledge, to enable them to be fully effective in their involvement with the new Trust. This led to the production of a plan outlining the needs of the area and describing a two-year capacity building programme. Bradford Task Force agreed to finance the Canterbury Partnership Trust with a of £85,000 as part of its 'exit strategy' before it closed in the autumn of 1995. The focus on capacity building was a key to obtaining the grant, seen by the Task Force as a useful link between community activity and improving the skills base in the area. The capacity building work on the estate has included a number of elements:

- a course-based training programme covering organisational and management skills

- action-based learning, for example on presentation skills and visits to other projects

- use of two consultants to assist with fund-raising and the development of estate-based working groups

- use of specialist architectural advice on the design of a new multi-purpose community building

- community work support over a four-year period to assist in the development of the People's Group and the Partnership Trust. The community worker is a CDF-funded post.

- assistance and support from the partnership manager based in the Housing Directorate.

The content of the capacity building work is described more fully later. Particular points to note from the work are:

- The capacity building initiative has been led by a grassroots community organisation that quite openly recognised a skills gap as they moved to involvement in a new more complex structure

'Our vision - empowerment and people in charge through training.'
The People's Group

- the capacity building plan developed in 1995 significantly strengthened the funding bid submitted to the Bradford Task Force. The potential use of capacity building plans is explored in Part 5

- capacity building is taking a variety of forms rather than just consisting of the more conventional course based training programme. The need for a variety of approaches to capacity building is one of the key themes explored in this publication

- there is a combination of ongoing community work support that existed for several years in advance of the more specific capacity building programmes; the relationship between community work and capacity building is discussed in Part 4.

For more information contact: The Canterbury Partnership Trust, telephone: 01274-52 2911.

Further reading

Association of Metropolitan Authorities (1993) *Local Authorities and Community Development: A Strategic Opportunity for the 1990s.*

Baine, S. (1994) *Building Community Partnerships: Good practice guidelines for local authorities, support for community organisations and community buildings,* Community Matters.

Butcher, H. Glen, A., Henderson, P., Smith, J. (1995) *Community and Public Policy,* Pluto Press/CDF/BICC.

CDF (1996) *Regeneration and the Community.*

Chanan, G. (1994) *Discovering Community Action,* CDF

Cheung-Judge, M-Y,. Henley, A. (1994) *Equality in Action,* NCVO.

Clarke, G. (1995) *A Missed Opportunity,* NCVO.

Cole, G. A. (1993) *Personnel Management,* DP Publications.

Craig, G. and Mayo, M. (1995) *Community Empowerment,* Zed Books.

Davis Smith, J., Rochester, C., and Hedley, R. (1995) *An Introduction to the Voluntary Sector,* Routledge

Department of the Environment (1992) *PA CEC: An evaluation of the Government's Inner Cities Task Force Initiative,* Vol 1, HMSO.

Department of the Environment (1994) *Inner Cities Research Programme Assessing the impact of urban policy,* HMSO.

Department of the Environment (1995) *Involving the Community in Urban and Rural Regeneration,* HMSO.

Dominelli, L. (1990) *Women and Community Action,* Venture Press.

Fordham, G. (1995) *Made to last: Creating sustainable neighbourhood and estate regeneration,* Joseph Rowntree Foundation.

Hall, S., Beazley, M., Bentley, G., Burfitt, A., Collinge, C., Lee, P., Loftman, P., Nevin, B., Srbljanin, A. (1996) *The Single Regeneration Budget. A review of the Challenge Fund Round Two,* Centre for Urban and Regional Studies, Birmingham University.

Hastings, A., McArthur, A., McGregor, A. (1996) *Less than Equal? Community organisations and estate regeneration partnerships,* Policy Press

Meekosha, H. (1993) '*The Bodies Politic'* in Butcher et al. (1995) *Community and Public Policy,* Pluto Press/CDF/BICC.

NCVO (1996) *Further to Go?,* NCVO Publications.

Taylor, M. (1995) *Unleashing the Potential: Bringing residents to the centre of regeneration,* Joseph Rowntree Foundation.

Thake, S. (1995) *Staying the Course: The role and structures of community regeneration organisations,* Policy Press.

Welsh Office, (1995) *Strategic Development Scheme,* Welsh Office Circular No 36/95.

Part 2
Developing People

Many community groups, in getting involved in decision making structures, managing local projects and initiating community enterprise, are recognising the need for learning programmes to further develop the skills, knowledge and abilities of their members. Yet in practice training provision is often unimaginative in form, usually course-based and organised with only a patchy assessment of individual and organisational needs.

The aims of Part 2 are to:

- explore a variety of forms of community-based training and learning, looking at the advantages and disadvantages of each form
- examine community-based training in the light of the themes of empowerment and equality
- give some practical guidelines on carrying out training needs analyses.

For both participants and regeneration agencies, community-based training can have at least three key benefits. Through increasing skill levels of individual group members, it increases the effectiveness of community organisations in pursuing their own aims and activities. In turn, it increases the ability of individuals and organisations to participate in consultations, partnerships and decision making, thus contributing to the successful implementation of the regeneration programme. Thirdly, by raising levels of skills, knowledge and confidence of individuals it may help people get paid work; in other words, community activity provides opportunities to learn new skills that are often transferable to the paid work environment.

To be effective, community-based training should be based on a review of training needs. In practice it is still not very often that community groups ask for help with identifying training needs. More often a request for training arises because of a crisis, a new problem or new opportunity – or because a course 'sounds interesting'! Rather than merely reacting in this way, training is much more effectively organised if it is part of a longer term look at the needs of both individuals and the organisation. Many groups are unfamiliar with training – let alone the idea of identifying training needs – and may need support in understanding its role.

In Part 2 we start with an examination of different forms of training, making a comparison of the advantages and disadvantages of each particular form. We then move on to explore the case for community-based training in terms of increased employability, and then discuss empowerment and equality as underlying principles in capacity building. Part 2 finishes with a section on practical guidelines for identifying training needs.

Terms and definitions

In order to avoid repetition, in this publication we now use the term 'skills' as a shorthand term to refer to the development of skills, knowledge, awareness, ability, aptitude and confidence.

The term 'training' is used consciously as a very broad term to refer to any learning activity, whether formal or informal, broadly associated with involvement in community development activities. 'Forms of learning' would be a more accurate description than 'forms of training' described here in Part 2; however the term 'learning' is not viewed as an accessible term for many community group members.

Forms of training

Training as an aspect of capacity building can take a variety of forms; in this section we examine different forms and debate the advantages and disadvantages of each one. Ideally the form of the training is only chosen once training needs have been established, using one or a combination of the methods described later in Part 2. The type of needs identified will obviously affect the choice of form the training would take.

Being aware of a variety of forms of training is important because people learn in different ways.

So why consider a range of forms of training? In planning and organising capacity building, being aware of a variety of forms of training is important because people learn in different ways (Honey and Mumford 1986). Course-based training – the most common form of provision – may suit some people while others may learn more effectively through direct experience or participation in a mentoring scheme. Also each form of training has its own advantages and disadvantages which need to be weighed up in relation to needs – and resources – in deciding which form to choose. The choice of form should be made in consultation with participants or potential participants wherever possible. So, here follows a description of a variety of forms of training; some are already widely used while others are less common and innovative.

Here follows a description of a variety of forms of training; some are already widely used while others are less common and innovative.

Group-based training

This is training that is designed and run specifically for an existing group who already know each other. Consequently, this type of training is usually provided in response to a request from the group and is tailor-made to their needs. It is usually held in the building the group normally uses and for convenience may even be held at the same time of day as a normal group meeting. The term 'group' here means management committee, steering group and so on.

Advantages

- Because the training happens in the building the group normally uses, there is a greater chance of more people being involved. Some group members may feel unconfident about visiting a local adult education

centre or college to go to a training event, yet would participate in one being held in familiar surroundings

- As well as addressing individual learning needs, by working with a whole group this form of training can easily lead on to or be a part of organisational development work. For example, a session on the roles and skills involved in committee work could lead on to a team building session to address tensions among group members that are blocking effective collaboration. For some groups this is a useful way to approach team building, framed within the less loaded context of a 'course' producing less resistance than if the problems were otherwise confronted head-on

- For groups whose first language is not English, the training can be carried out in their own common language. This is a particular advantage, for example, in capacity building work with refugee groups.

Disadvantages

- Some groups may be stuck in a rather inward looking culture that prohibits new learning. Mixing with members of other groups may be a more effective form of learning

- Because the training happens in the group's usual meeting venue and even at the usual day and time, it may not be taken seriously enough or may become dominated by business items – or noisy interruptions

- By being group-based, the training is not an opportunity to meet other groups and form new links. Training that involves several groups can be an effective networking tool

- Because the content is designed specifically for the group rather than being course-based it will probably mean it will not be part of an accredited course. Consequently, participants' work does not contribute to any form of qualification. Issues around qualifications and accreditation are discussed later.

Despite these disadvantages, group-based training has a crucial role to play in capacity building. The key feature of its effectiveness is that it provides tailor-made content for the particular needs of the group. It is also a useful opportunity to recognise and identify existing skills, experience and knowledge the group already has. For many community groups it is their first contact with training and because of understandable fears around 'education' may for many participants be the only initial route into adult learning.

Course-based training

Course-based training is usually held in a more central venue and involves members from several community groups and organisations in a network or area. It usually takes the form of a pre-set course, participation in which may contribute to gaining a qualification. To achieve this, the course itself will need to be accredited; examples of particular relevance to capacity building are given later.

Advantages

- Because on the course participants are drawn from a number of groups there will be a wider range of experience and perspectives to share and learn from compared to group-based training

- Because the course may contain some content not specifically requested by any one individual, it may introduce participants to new, useful ideas and skills they might not otherwise have experienced

- Because people are away from their familiar surroundings, they may be more open to new experiences and ideas

- When the course is accredited, participants may obtain a qualification or recognition of learning that contributes to a qualification. We explore this later.

Disadvantages

- Because it is a pre-set course, some of the content may not be of interest to some participants. Obviously, effective teaching in this setting is about relating the content to participants' own experience and interests, though the increasing move to accredited course provision may reduce this flexibility

- When held in a central venue it may only attract people who can travel there easily

- When held in a central venue, course-based training may only attract participants who are already reasonably skilled and confident. In turn, these participants may not pass on new learning effectively to other group members, although this issue can be addressed during the course.

- If the course-based provision is linked to a system of assessment, this may alienate and reduce the involvement of people unfamiliar with the process.

As you can see, course-based and group-based training have contrasting advantages and disadvantages. For course-based provision, some of the problems associated with distant or unfamiliar venues can be alleviated by holding a course in an estate based community centre, though this may then reduce the numbers attending from other estates. Group-based work is viewed by some training organisations only as a form of outreach, a stepping stone to encourage later participation in more structured and institutionally based provision. But group-based training is also a powerful form of learning in its own right and especially effective when linked to organisational change. It can be an important element in capacity building programmes that aim to involve minority groups who feel alienated by mainstream provision – sessions can be carefully tailored not only to specific learning needs but also to the social and cultural setting of the group. With the growing availability of the individual accreditation of learning, for example, through NVQs, group-based training can also increasingly be seen as an accessible route to gaining qualifications.

Course-based training

Examples of useful accredited courses for members of community organisations

Running Community Buildings

A course for management committees running or developing community centres, village halls and similar community buildings. Three modules cover Planning and Development, Running and Managing, and Relating to the Community and Equal Opportunities. The course is accredited nationally through the Open College Network and can attract Further Education Funding Council finance.
Contact: Community Matters, 0113 2456634.

Introductory Community Work Skills

Courses are run by members of the Federation of Community Work Training Groups and others, and adapted to the needs of each region. Most courses are successfully accredited through the Open College Network and are then entitled to FEFC funding under Schedule 2 of the funding guidelines. This Stage One Introductory Course forms an important point of entry for local people into community work; Stage Two Community Work Skills Courses leading to a Certificate have also been developed, but to date only in Manchester, Leeds and Glasgow.
Contact: FCWTG, telephone: 0114 2739391.

Community Work S/NVQ

Over the past five years, extensive development work has been carried out, involving over 1,000 community workers across the UK to establish new occupational standards for community work. This has resulted in awards at three levels: S/NVQ Level Two Community Activist, S/NVQ Level Three Community Assistant/Activist/Worker, and S/NVQ Level Four Community Work Manager. To date the awarding bodies are CCETSW, BTEC, City and Guilds and SCOTVEC. Remember although often linked to course provision, NVQs are essentially a form of assessment.
Contact: FCWTG, telephone: 0114 2739391.

RSA Advanced Diploma in the Organisation of Community Groups

This is a basic management qualification suitable for people who have experience of committee work and running a group. The award is flexible in delivery, consisting of nine units, including managing physical, financial and human resources, administration and organising, working with groups and maintaining external relations. Centres running the award scheme vary in their own levels of experience in and links with community work.
Contact: RSA Examinations Board, telephone: 01203 468080

Training for Community Consultants Course

This course aims to develop the knowledge, skills and confidence of participants so that they can act more effectively as community consultants with the management committees of community organisations and groups. It is aimed at volunteers and paid workers who have substantial experience of working with community organisations. The course is accredited under the Middlesex University Academic Credit Scheme and is run in various parts of Britain by Community Matters.
Contact: Community Matters, telephone: 0171-226 0189

Action-based learning

Action-based learning takes place when a group consciously undertakes a process of reflecting upon and reviewing their own activity in order to clearly identify and draw out what has been learnt from their experience, and how such learning can be used to improve future practice. It is an important tool for development and should be seen not as an alternative to other forms of training described in this section but as an ongoing process which can over time become an integral part of the way a group functions.

Action-based learning involves focusing on a specific activity the group has been involved in and working through a sequence of questions to draw out the learning. These could be:

- what were the objectives of the activity?

- what objectives did we achieve and how?

- what were the difficulties and problems we encountered?

- why did these occur and how could we have overcome them?

- how would we do things differently in the future?

Action-based learning works best when carried out as soon as possible after the activity being focused on, when the experience is still 'live' in people's memories. Although the process can be undertaken by the group without 'outside' facilitation there may be difficult issues to explore or internal conflicts over any difficulties encountered, which can be more productively worked through with the help of a third party. This may be a local community worker or a facilitator brought in to guide and help the group through the process and help resolve any differences. Once the group has understood the process it will be able to build it in as an integral part of its activities. It is important that action-based learning should not just focus on difficulties but also serve to evaluate and celebrate successes and achievements.

Action-based learning is also an important approach to help groups look at the wider social context of their activity, exploring the causes and nature of deprivation and discrimination. This approach as has been used by many women community development workers in working with women in communities: 'The idea is that this reflection helped women come up with their own collective analysis of the situations that caused those experiences and to move on from there to consider what action should be taken to deal with or challenge those situations' (FCWTG 1994).

Advantages

- A real life and immediate exercise in learning from experience

- as an approach, it enables negative experiences to be immediately explored and be seen as productive and positive

- it recognises and validates the group's own experience and provides a way to give immediate and positive feedback for individual and collective achievement

'You can train until you are blue in the face but there is no substitute for direct experience.'
Senior manager,
City Challenge

'The choice of form of training should be made in consultation with participants or potential participants wherever possible.'
Community work manager

- it provides opportunity for 'rounding off' activity in a positive and developmental way to build for the future.

Disadvantages

- Without sensitive handling, wounds can be deepened rather than healed
- it relies upon all those who have had a key involvement in the activity being able to participate
- it is limited in its potential for drawing new people into activity.

Consortium-based learning

In consortium-based learning members of a number of community organisations join together to form a learning group with the assistance of a facilitator. Ideally, each community organisation sends two or three members with the full commitment of the management committee to in turn share and benefit from their experience. Consortiums can have at least three main roles for effective learning:

- exchange of information, ideas, experience and skills between participants
- participation in a tailor-made or accredited course specifically run for the consortium
- collective activities such as starting a jointly run community enterprise or working on a joint funding application.

Obviously the roles can vary over time as the confidence and familiarity of the group grows. The first two roles – information exchange and course participation – can form a solid base for collective initiatives. The latter can still be an opportunity for learning where the facilitator encourages reflection, evaluation of experience and task-oriented skill development.

If a consortium is to engage in the third action-oriented role, this initiative will need to be carefully negotiated with members' own organisations so that the joint activity complements rather than threatens their existing aims and objectives (McEachrane, Lee, Parish and Clark, 1994).

Based on the experience of the Local Economic Consortium, described below, learning is more effective when members represent a range of different stages in terms of organisational development. Reviews of consortium progress can be built in allowing a change of membership as appropriate, based on the approval of all existing members.

Advantages

- Consortium-based learning relies on the active exchange of skills between members. This activity is a valuable recognition of the wealth of skill, experience and talent that exists in the community sector, and itself as a process can be a real confidence boost for the participants
- The action orientation of the consortium model can be a powerful learning opportunity where participants learn through involvement in collective rather than individual initiatives

• Consortiums, involving by definition members of a number of organisations, can help to establish new relationships and effective sharing of resources.

Disadvantages

• Involvement in the third role of joint activities requires a much larger investment of time and skill both for the consortium facilitator and the members. A collective initiative, such as a joint grant application, will have to be carefully organised with the full approval of each member organisation and an appropriate system of communication and management established.

Case Study: Consortium-Based Learning

The Local Economic Consortium, London

The Local Economic Consortium is made up of a membership of eight black, ethnic minority and refugee organisations. It was established with technical management assistance and consultancy support from a consultancy agency called Capacity Unlimited, who combined joint economic initiatives with a structured learning programme. The key to its success was that the decision to join the consortium was made in each case by the management or executive committee of each organisation, who in turn identified appropriate staff and committed their time to the consortium's activities. This involved development work with each organisation to help reduce potential blocks to consortium formation. These blocks were a lack of awareness of what the consortium model of learning and economic initiatives could provide, and fears about possible loss of control through the formation of a new collective body.

It also involved working with the organisations to:

- establish membership criteria

- help to clarify a mission statement for the consortium and clearly define roles and responsibilities

- agree on the consortium's structure, i.e. how decisions are made and who carries them out.

Once established, the LEC became a lively and very valuable forum for exchange and learning. Participants shared their own particular skill and knowledge and arranged to share specialist information in theme based sessions when needed, for example on NVQs. Over three years, Capacity Unlimited ran two main training courses:

- an initial course in capacity building to deliver economic development initiatives

- a fuller programme on local economic development and organisational development.

At all times over the three years, there has been a mixture of a training input and the exchange of skill and knowledge between participants. Participation on these courses also means participants can obtain accreditation through the Open University.

Some key points from the work of LEC are:

- The consortium was established with an explicit aim of joint economic development initiatives as well as providing a learning network. Effective involvement was

assisted by a process of clear agenda setting, enabling the understanding and ownership of participating organisations. Without this clarity and initial development work, especially given the range of roles involved in consortium collaboration, there is the potential for confusion and later difficulties

- To be effective for the joint activities role, consortiums need to be established with a long-term commitment. Operational guidelines on how the member organisations will relate to each other and engage in joint management need to be established before grant applications or trading activities are initiated. In contrast, consortiums formed for the sole pursuit of funding may be short-lived and lacking in organisational base to continue

- In particular where joint activity is a main part of a consortium's aims, training has a crucial role to bring all participants to a shared level of understanding of managerial needs and similar level of organisational skills. Establishing such a broad parity was seen as a key benefit of the training programme to provide a solid baseline for later joint initiatives.

LEC's innovative work has fed into the National Development Agenda project whose main aim is to promote the establishment of local economic development strategies within local communities. This project has also involved the National Council for Voluntary Organisations and the Black Training and Enterprise Group.

For more information contact: Local Economic Consortium Management Services, telephone: 0171-226 0085.

Community mentoring

Mentoring is a system of one-to-one support and learning usually carried out within one organisation. In community mentoring the mentoring happens between individuals who are based in two different organisations. There are two main forms of community mentoring, dependent on the type of organisation from where the mentor originates:

• business sector organisations

• well-established voluntary or community sector organisations.

In both cases, the mentoring support is given to an individual who is based in a less well-established voluntary or community sector organistion, though business based mentoring schemes have also included 'mentees' based in schools and colleges. Mentors and mentees are usually linked together through a process of matching, organised by a scheme co-ordinator.

The matching criteria can include:

• the appropriate technical skills of the mentor

• their personality and communication skills

• their interests and backgrounds in relation to those of the mentee.

The mentoring relationship in this context can involve at least three aspects, with the first aspect usually being dominant:

- guidance and advice giving
- the facilitation of learning
- support and confidence building.

Some mentoring schemes, for example one run in Bethnal Green City Challenge, also involve the mentor in hands-on practical work with the mentee. In some cases it can also involve work with the whole management committee, not just the individual mentee.

'Mentoring is especially important for young black people in capacity building to provide black role models.'
The Oxford Conference

The aims of community mentoring can be to:

- increase the skill and confidence level of the individual mentees
- improve the effectiveness of the recipient organisation
- encourage a sharing of knowledge, skills and experience between community and voluntary organisations
- facilitate networking links between the community, voluntary and, where appropriate, business sector
- help mentors to develop their interpersonal skills and awareness of the needs of the community sector.

Practice points

The Hackney Community Mentoring Scheme is described below in a case study. Some key points from this work are:

- Mentee organisations need to be involved with a full commitment to the learning process so that new skills and knowledge is shared rather than remaining solely with the individual mentee. This is especially important to avoid a loss of benefit if the mentee moves on from the organisation at a later point. This involvement is also needed to ensure the mentee's time commitment and additional support does not create resentment
- The roles between mentor and mentee need to be clearly established through proper induction and support. For example, the mentee must be clear that the mentor is not there to 'solve all their problems' or act as a 'doer' rather than mentor. This involves the equivalent of a day's training for both the mentor and mentee.

Advantages

'With one all-male group, we intentionally placed a female mentor as a role model to challenge their assumptions about women.'
Mentor scheme organiser

- Mentoring is a form of intensive learning and facilitation for individuals based in an organisational setting. The nature of the relationship can encourage the mentee to explore their own personal blocks to learning and change through a degree of one-to-one support that is usually unavailable in course-based training
- Where the source of the mentor is another voluntary or in particular a community organisation, mentoring is a valuable way of recognising the wealth of skills in the community and voluntary sector. A key feature is that it can provide role models of more successful organisations
- The personal and organisational links arising from the mentoring relationship can often lead to ongoing networking and shared activities;

such partnerships are especially useful when they outlive the lifespan of the regeneration agency.

Disadvantages

- Community mentoring is a resource intensive approach to learning. The process of setting up the scheme, matching organisations and giving ongoing support requires considerable staff time input.

Other models of community mentoring

- In Sheffield on the Manor Estate, an established residents' group regularly helps a less experienced group with advice and guidance. This is a useful alternative to a more resource-intensive form of community mentoring. Such arrangements can be very valuable form of support even without systematic matching and explicit agreements, though if not clearly based on a one-to-one relationship may be better defined as a form of networking rather than mentoring. However it is defined, it has valuable potential and a variety of forms of organisation. *For more information contact: Manor Training and Resource Centre, telephone: 0114 2642194.*

- In Birmingham, five community-based Credit Unions with common borders have formed a group offering support and advice to newly-developing credit unions (Brush, unpublised). Again such inter-group arrangements may not have the careful matching and support of the more structured schemes but are certainly cheaper to set up and may still produce some effective skill sharing and networking.

- In Leeds, the Work and Learning Club run by the Belle Isle Foundation, a community organisation, is involved in an innovative form of mentoring in particular making use of TEC funding. The club uses outreach and community networks to contact long term unemployed people and assists them by providing mentors, to devise and carry out short term projects. Projects enable people to develop confidence, contacts and skills. Ideas for each project comes from each individual involved; examples include setting up a co-operative to repair bicycles; selling wholefoods; finding out about skills needed to write stories; or a project to improve parenting skills that leads to training in child care. Outcomes agreed with the funders of the scheme, Leeds TEC, include entry into further education, training uptake, employment and increased community involvement. The first year's experience of running the scheme has demonstrated the importance of effective mentoring. *For more information contact the Belle Isle Foundation, telephone: 0113 2716139.*

- In Bradford, the Royds Community Association, an SRB funded Partnership, has established a traineeship scheme to train six local people in community work skills. Each participant is matched with a practising community worker in one of the three areas the Royds programme covers. They offer mentoring and support, based on a three-year learning contract. Participants also attend accredited community work training courses commissioned by the Royds Community Association and run locally. *For more information contact: Royds Community Association, telephone: 01274 772273.*

Case Study:
Community Mentoring

The Hackney Community Mentoring Scheme

This case study describes an innovative mentoring programme established in Hackney. The scheme was established as a pilot programme in 1995, involving five mentors and five mentees, all based in voluntary and community organisations across the borough. The mentor's role is to work with individuals from community groups which need assistance in the following areas:

- fund-raising and finance

- managing staff

- community consultations and public meetings

- equal opportunities

- strategic planning.

Involvement in the scheme is based on an agreement that:

- mentors and mentees have at least five hours contact per month

- both organisations involved in the relationship need to give their approval and commitment

- the mentoring sessions are confidential, with mutual respect between both participants

- there is a process of evaluation against stated objectives.

The Hackney programme was developed because it was recognised that some organisations in the borough – especially newer, less established groups – needed forms of support unavailable through conventional training. The scheme was organised by East London Community Training, building on their work in community mentoring on the Isle of Dogs. The earlier project had led to the following outcomes:

- some mentees progressing on to further training courses, for exampl the Open University

- some mentees using their learning for accreditation on NVQ Level II in Management

- some mentees in turn becoming mentors to other organisations

- some mentors themselves further pursuing their own personal an professional development.

Building on this experience, the Hackney scheme was set up through:

- A mass mail-out to voluntary and community organisations as potential mentors and mentees, inviting them to a launch and presentation evening

- Interviews of those organisations showing interest. Potential mentors were assessed and a needs analysis carried out of the potential mentee's organisation

- Out of 20 organisations interviewed ten were selected creating five pairs of mentors and mentees. Mentee organisations were selected on the basis of those most in need of assistance

- The matching process considered not just appropriate skills but how the background and personal skills of the mentor might both support and, at times, challenge the mentee to enable their growth and change. This is in contrast to allowing a self-selection process of matching which could leave participants with

a less challenging relationship. For example, a male-dominated theatre group was allocated an experienced female arts administrator and training director.

Practical arrangements

After introductory meetings and an induction phase, mentors and mentees make their own arrangements to meet, in terms of times and location. Face-to-face meetings are supplemented with back-up telephone contact. The co-ordinator offers ongoing support if needed and facilitates both a mid-term and final review and evaluation. With five matched pairs, this support involved work from a co-ordinator for over a day a week. The Hackney scheme is a six-month long programme and mentor organisations receive payment at £30 per hour for mentor contact time and expenses. This was seen as appropriate, especially as mentors were usually at senior managerial level in their own organisations.

The Hackney Community Mentoring Programme was co-ordinated by East London Community Training. It was jointly funded by Dalston City Partnership, Hackney Task Force, Hackney TEC and Hackney Borough Council. ELCT wishes to acknowledge that their approach was built on work developed by Roots and Wings.

For more information on the Hackney Community Mentoring Scheme contact: East London Community Training, telephone: 0171-512 3000

For information on business-based community mentoring schemes contact: Roots and Wings at Business in the Community, telephone: 0171-224 1600.

Placements

Placements are a little-used form of learning in capacity building, yet have great potential. A volunteer participant is placed with an outside organisation to learn skills through observation and specific activities, guided by a link staff member. Placements may last from a few days to an extensive period over a few months. For example, a member of a community group involved in campaigns spends a day a week over five weeks on placement at a local commercial printers. Here the participant may not only learn about the processes involved in artwork preparation and printing, but also useful practical skills for designing leaflets.

Such placements need a clear agreement as to roles and support, as well as liability on health and safety issues. Often a major concern of the host organisation is that the placement will take up too much time and work activities involve too much supervision. In some cases, observation rather than active involvement may be more suitable, yet can still be very effective. A key to effective learning is that the participant and the link staff member establish a good relationship, with clear and supportive communication.

Advantages

With appropriate support and supervision, an outside placement can be a valuable learning experience and for a long-term unemployed person, may provide an informal insight into work environments.

Disadvantages

The system is based on a lone individual visiting and interacting in an outside organisation; without appropriate support this can be a difficult experience and, for individuals low on confidence, may be even quite stressful.

Secondments and volunteers

Here a staff member from a larger organisation is seconded or volunteers to work with a host community group. Such volunteers and secondees, depending on their background, can offer:

- general business, administrative and organisational skills
- specialist skills, such as computing or bookkeeping
- project design and management skills
- contacts and introductions.

Business in the Community organises a variety of schemes involving volunteers and secondments from the private sector:

- *Transitional Secondments* can last from three months to two years full time where the employing company continues to pay the salary and the employee fulfils a particular role within the host organisation.
- *Development Assignments* usually last 100 hours and are typically spread out as one day over 13 weeks. These short-term secondments are aimed at developing the skills and confidence of employees from companies, as well as providing benefits to the community organisation
- *Business Volunteers* are usually individual volunteers from companies who offer specific skills or expertise. They can provide advice and support, for example on computers, finance or training. Projects need to be one-off and clearly defined
- *Business on Board* is a Business in the Community initiative, to encourage people from companies to join boards of not-for-profit organisations.

Secondments and volunteering schemes can be especially effective when:

- Secondees and volunteers are chosen carefully so that the group achieves some lasting benefits
- There is a clear agreement on the volunteer's or secondee's role, work area, contact person and support from the group
- The volunteer's or secondee's contribution is time-limited, with a plan to pass on skills enabling the group's own members whenever possible to carry on the work after secondment
- There is a final stage of review and appreciation of their contribution as appropriate.

There are obvious benefits to the community organisation in the use of volunteers and secondments. In addition the volunteers and secondees will benefit in different ways. For example, they may gain greater insight into participative forms of group organisation. They may also gain some under-

standing of problems experienced in deprived communities, as well as experience of working with a grassroots, committed organisation. In other words, the relationship should not be seen as just a one-way benefit.

'Surprisingly few people challenge the use of private sector models and assumptions when transferred to the voluntary and community sector.'
Lecturer in management studies

Volunteers and secondees will also need to be aware that many community groups run in an informal participatory style – the volunteers or secondees will need to be flexible in their approach. Another issue to consider is that community development has a value-base that is not and should not be finance driven; often business models and assumptions imported fresh from the private sector will not be appropriate without adaptation and review.

Advantages

- A secondment or voluntary involvement from a person with specialist skills who works in a flexible manner can be very useful to a community organisation. Where the secondee is working with several group members it can provide a learning opportunity for a number of people, compared to the one-to-one relationship involved in mentoring.

Disadvantages

- Without awareness of the value base of community development, business-based secondees and volunteers may unconsciously transfer inappropriate models and assumptions to their work with community sector organisations.

Business in the Community (BiTC)

BiTC is a national not-for-profit organisation whose mission is to support the social and economic regeneration of communities, by raising the quality and extent of business involvement and by making that involvement a natural part of successful business practice. BiTC staff, based in a network of regional offices, can advise and help to broker certain forms of private sector support to aid community organisations including mentoring schemes, secondments and volunteer schemes. *For more information contact: Business in the Community, telephone: 0171-224 1600.*

Exchange visits

Exchange visits are an important addition or alternative to group and course-based training because groups learn directly from each other. This process may build up confidence about taking initiatives more than the same information being transmitted by a trainer. While this is the case, exchange visits obviously still need to be carefully organised in order to be effective, either by a paid worker or by group members.

Exchange visit is the term frequently used for an inter-organisation visit, though rarely in practice is the visit two-way. More often a party of people from one community organisation visits another organisation where they perceive that the organisation can help them in their own development. To be effective, exchange visits need:

- careful preparation – that the aim of the visit is clear to both organisations; that all available information about the host organisation is given to participants prior to the visit

- good organisation – attention given to practical details of child care, transport, access and catering, so that the event is equally accessible to all potential participants

- systematic follow-up – a session to share reactions to the visit, identify key learning points and implications for action.

Disadvantages

- Without adequate communication and planning, visits can become merely sightseeing tours with little real learning

- In some cases the host organisation uses the visit as a public relations exercise to impress outside organisations rather than, for example, to share the difficulties experienced in reaching their achievements. Equally, if the host organisation is significantly more developed and established than the visiting organisation, this large gap can be demoralising rather than inspiring.

'When we made our visit to the development trust, we weren't even shown around but just given a lecture about how wonderful it all was.'
Community activist

Advantages

- A key advantage is that the group is learning directly from and being supported by another group or community organisation. This can inspire a 'we can do that too' belief which can be a major boost to group morale

- Visits may lead on to the formation of ongoing links between groups and organisations, which can contribute to joint campaigning or joint capacity building programmes.

Summary

This review of different forms of training has demonstrated that a variety of options are available. There are others that have an important role to play that we have not had space to explore, for example:

- theme-based discussion groups

- supported reading programmes

- shadowing, i.e. observation of and joint working with more experienced group members

- computer-based distance learning.

Awareness of a range of options is important if capacity building is carried out in a way that is systematic, comprehensive and forward looking. As described at the start of this section, it is also more effective to consider the use of a variety of forms of training because evidence suggests adults learn in different ways; drawing on a variety of options is also important because of different cultural backgrounds of participants. In particular practitioners and programme managers need to be aware that for any one group, capacity building needs and the appropriate form of training may change and develop over time. Fledgling groups may need different forms of help compared to well-established organisations, and groups attempting to take on new roles and structures may need more intensive levels of support. These issues are explored more fully in Part 5.

Case study:
The Canterbury Partnership Trust, Bradford

This case study demonstrates the effective use of a variety of forms of training by a community-based development trust. As described in Part 1, the Peoples' Group, a grassroots residents' association, has now formed a Partnership Trust and invited representatives from the local authority, police, private sector, churches and education to join the board. The aims of the trust are to act as a co-ordinating body for local initiatives, to bring in new resources and to become a strong voice in representing the area.

Residents' representatives have the majority of places on the board and believe it is important that they have the skills and knowledge to manage the trust, working jointly but not dominated by the other non-resident members. In order to achieve this the People's Group has developed a two-year capacity building plan, based on an initial review of training needs. The proposed content of this training programme includes:

- publicity and presentation skills
- assertion training and confidence building
- fund-raising and managing money
- understanding jargon and how the council works
- building the group, dealing with conflict and supporting volunteers
- community work and training skills
- word processing and report writing.

Over the last year a variety of forms of training have been used to respond to different needs and interests:

- *Course-based training.* The Tenants' Participation Advisory Service (TPAS) has been commissioned to run an open short course-based in the community centre, covering many of the skill areas listed. Course-based provision has also included a Stage 1 community work skills course being run on the estate by Bradford and Ilkley Community College

- *Group-based training.* Tailor made training sessions have been run by a fund-raising adviser for group members on fund-raising skills

- *Action-based learning.* A major launch presentation in the city hall was used by the group as a way to identify and learn presentation skills. This included preparation and review sessions organised with support from the centre-based community worker

- *Visits.* The group has visited other projects and a development trust, in order to broaden members' understanding of estate-based initiatives

- *Professional advice.* The Professional Firms Group scheme provided architectural advice to assist in the design of a new multi-purpose community building.

This combination of training forms, with an emphasis on it being needs-led and locally-based, is proving to be a useful way to organise capacity building. Some residents who are becoming involved in learning new skills and knowledge would have felt uncertain about participating in courses run by a college or adult education centre.

*For more information contact: the Canterbury Partnership Trust,
telephone: 01274 522911.*

Employability

Increasingly, many activists, volunteers and community group members want improved employment prospects as a benefit of their involvement in community activity.

Regeneration agencies are also seeing capacity building based around community involvement increasingly as a useful bridge for introducing 'non-traditional learners' to employment-related vocational training. For example, Bradford Task Force – in continuing funding for the Canterbury Partnership Trust, whose two-year action plan included an extensive capacity building programme – specifically based the decision on these considerations.

In this section we examine in turn three main ways in which capacity building that is primarily focused on community activities can also contribute to increased employability. These are the acquisition of transferable skills, opportunities for qualifications and accreditation, and involvement in community economic development. Another key link is the general increase in personal confidence that can arise from involvement in community activities, although this point is explored later, in the section on empowerment.

To be effective, the training route to increased employability needs to be complemented by a range of other approaches that specifically address blocks to employment commonly experienced by residents in regeneration areas. We now examine the three links between capacity building and increased employability.

Transferable skills

Many of the skills, abilities and knowledge learnt in the arena of community activity can be transferred into workplace environments. Obviously, the degree of transferability will vary depending on the nature of the employment and the occupational area. Here are some examples of skill and knowledge development common to the activities of many community organisations that may be directly transferable into workplace environments:

- Communication skills such as publicity, public speaking, delegation and feedback skills, chairing meetings
- Management skills such as financial control, planning use of resources and space, monitoring and evaluation, recruitment and selection of staff
- Teamwork skills an area increasingly sought after by many progressive employers and especially useful in co-operative based community economic development
- Organisational skills such as running a playscheme, co-ordinating a community festival, running a network, arranging a public meeting
- Practical skills such as keyboard and word processing skills, book keeping, surveying, production of newsletters.

Blocks to the effective transfer of such skills are:

- People not recognising their own skill levels, especially when derived from less formal settings, for example running a playscheme
- Employers being narrow-minded to the value of skills developed in a voluntary context
- Employers only being prepared to recognise skills when they are identified within a recognised qualification.

Qualifications and accreditation

We now move on to examine the second key link between capacity building and increased employability of local people.

It is useful to build into the organisation of training in capacity building appropriate arrangements for the accreditation and recognition of individual learning. The advantages arising from this are:

- One of the increasingly common questions asked by participants on local training courses over recent years has been 'what qualification or certification do I receive on completing this course?'
- It will help participants to take full advantage of the increasing awareness by educational institutions and employers that community and voluntary activity is an important source of development for a wide range of knowledge and skills, and a key access point to further learning and education
- It can help to provide access to educational funding such as the Further Education Funding Council, which has been increasingly channelled into 'vocational' and accredited training courses.

These potential benefits need to be weighed up against three key considerations:

- Do the requirements for individual assessment shift the balance and focus of the training programme and divert the group from their primary learning objectives?
- Do requirements of accrediting or awarding bodies necessitate changes to the length, methods or content of courses, which may result in the course being less accessible or less clearly focused on the expressed needs of the participants?
- Does the organisation running the training have the resources and skills to provide the necessary individual support to participants?

Despite these reservations, the needs and aspirations of participants should be respected. Changes and developments over recent years have resulted in the growth of new vocational qualifications – National and Scottish Vocational Qualifications – and new arrangements and opportunities for accrediting locally-based training courses described below. This changing climate presents both opportunities and threats for those seeking to develop training for community organisations

In conclusion, there is a lot to consider in relation to accreditation and qualification. It is important to be aware not only of national developments and opportunities but also of the situation in your area. Even if you decide not to directly provide accreditation or qualification through your own training programmes you may be able to enable those individuals that wish to use it as a stepping stone to other opportunities.

National Vocational Qualifications

N/SVQs are being gradually developed in all occupational areas and provide qualifications based not on just what has been learnt, but on one's ability to provide evidence of competent practice. This can include both practice as a paid worker and practice as a volunteer or unpaid worker.

There are now N/SVQs in areas such as Play Work, Community Work, Training and Development, and Management and Administration. N/SVQs are broken down into 'units' where each unit describes a coherent area of activity. Where appropriate an Occupational Award will include units already developed. So, for example, the Community Work Awards include units from Management, Administration, Sports and Recreation and Training and Development. In this way recognition and qualification is given to transferable skills.

It is important to stress that N/SVQs are not training courses but that training is an important component of any N/SVQ programme.

The Open College Network
One of the most common and appropriate forms of gaining accreditation for learning obtained through community-based training is that provided by the National Open College Network. This network is made up of regional Open College organisations operating throughout England, Wales and Northern Ireland. Open Colleges do not at present offer national awards but 'credits', which participants can build up to enable them to access both further education and employment. To obtain credits individuals need to participate in a course recognised by the OCN which must have a minimum of 30 hours' 'notional learning time'.

The OCN gives course organisers the freedom and responsibility for developing their own course proposals including content, methods and assessment processes. Submissions are then considered by a recognition panel, involving those organising similar courses in the region. All submissions are related to agreed guidelines for all NOCN members.

Involvement in community economic development
There are a variety of forms of community economic development including:

- community enterprises
- worker based co-operatives
- credit unions
- development trusts

- trading activities linked to community buildings, for example a bar or café
- service delivery run by a community organisation, for example vocational training.

There is an obvious overlap between the skills and experience needed to run an effective community organisation and those involved in participating in community economic development. This is especially the case because community and voluntary sector organisations are part of a 'contract culture' environment and are increasingly involved in business planning and tight financial management. Case study evidence suggests that community economic activities develop more easily in areas that already have active community centres, community associations or community education projects. Apart from specific skills, involvement in community organisations can give participants experience in team work, practical organising and personal confidence in risk-taking, all of which can be strengthened through capacity building and are useful for involvement in community economic activity.

As you can see there is a strong argument available to regeneration agencies – should it be necessary – to justify capacity building training programmes in terms of the increased employability of participants. However if this route to increased opportunities for paid employment is a realistic one it needs to be complemented by a range of other approaches that specifically address blocks to employment commonly experienced by residents in regeneration areas.

These blocks may be, for example:
- racist attitudes among some employers towards certain minorities
- inadequate transport facilities
- inadequate child care provision which prevents lone parents in particular from working
- low pay which makes it uneconomic for people with families to come off benefit.

There are obviously many other well-known barriers to employability in regeneration areas; however unless at least some of these are being tackled by regeneration agencies, potential participants in training may feel understandably suspicious that increased employability is a likely outcome.

Empowerment

In this section of Part 2 we examine two key themes related to training as a part of community development and regeneration.

As shown in the earlier section, there are a variety of forms of training in capacity building which can be used as different options when planning training provision. However to be effective, this provision itself needs to be based on the two key principles of empowerment and equality. These

two principles are a useful framework within which to consider how community-based training is organised.

In the past, many regeneration agencies have focused on the employability aspect of capacity building and neglected the empowerment aspect. This is especially the case when the outputs from capacity building programmes are defined in specific numerical terms. Equally, empowerment as a term has become widely used, though often as an 'add on' label, often applied without much understanding or commitment. We believe empowerment is an essential underlying principle to any capacity building programme and that this has practical implications for both the methods and content of training. These are now explored and examined.

Defining empowerment

There are at least three different definitions of empowerment:

- *Empowerment as a process of increasing influence and control.* In this approach, empowerment can be seen as a process of delegating power, enabling a group to have more direct control over its own resources. A further development of this, within a 'ladder of participation' is where the group has an increasing degree of influence over decisions concerning not just its own resources but the allocation of resources and services locally (Wilcox 1994).

- *Empowerment as a psychological experience.* Here it is defined as an enabling process that leads to the development of a strong sense of personal effectiveness. In this approach, practical empowerment could include efforts to remove the feeling of powerlessness and involve elements that specifically build up confidence and self-esteem (Hopson and Scally 1981).

- *Empowerment as a process of analysing and understanding the causes of deprivation and discrimination.* This approach often takes inspiration from popular education initiatives developed in many Third World countries, often influenced by the work of Paulo Friere. It can include exploring the dynamics of discrimination and how people internalise negative messages about their status and rights (Eade and Williams 1995).

Practical implications

Each of these approaches to defining empowerment has a useful contribution to make to understanding the term; we now examine the practical implications of these three approaches to capacity building.

Empowerment as an underlying principle has a fundamental impact upon both the methods and content of community-based training. Here are some examples:

Impact on methods: participative training

To contribute to empowerment, training needs to be based on participative methods. The participative approach to training uses techniques and methods that encourage maximum involvement of all participants, for example through the use of small group exercises. Learning can be seen as a shared process with the trainer partly acting as a facilitator. A large part of the training would be to focus on and encourage the sharing and exchange of

'Because of the empowerment principle, for me capacity building is an approach underlying all our programmes.'
Assistant chief executive, City Challenge

the participants' own skills and ideas. This is more than just saying adults learn more effectively when the activities relate to their own experience – it's that their existing grassroots experience is of value in its own right (Skinner 1992).

It also involves a high degree of involvement in deciding on the content of the training, as described in the section on identifying training needs. This means that potential participants can choose the general area and level of the content and make informed choices about their involvement in accredited courses. Even where the course is accredited and the qualification is subject to the completion of a set syllabus, participative training methods can still be used to draw out and build on participants' existing skills and experience.

'Whatever form of training is used, people need to have a sense of ownership.'
Training organiser

Impact on content: personal development

The empowerment principle naturally leads to seeing personal development as a key part of any effective community-based training programme; this also complements the increased employability role described above. As described, the individual's own psychological experience of becoming more personally effective is an important aspect of empowerment. Personal development activities could include training and support on:

- identifying personal skills
- assertiveness and confidence building
- anti-sexism and anti-racism
- counselling and personal goal setting
- the nature of power and powerlessness
- inter-personal communication skills
- team work and conflict resolution.

While these activities focus on the individual, the emphasis can be on the person's own development in relation to their effective involvement in collective initiatives – capacity building is not concerned primarily with personal growth *per se*, but the individual in the context of group involvement and collective working. It is more a case of recognising the personal aspects of involvement in collective action which, without some attention and support, may act as a barrier to fuller participation.

Impact on content: understanding discrimination and deprivation

Training that focuses exclusively on the practical and technical areas of skill and knowledge involved in community organising would not contribute enough towards effective capacity building. The training needs also to encourage individuals to look critically at and understand processes that contribute to deprivation and discrimination. Examples of this are:

Action-based learning

- As part of a community profile, residents compile a history of their estate and the various improvement initiatives carried out over the last 20 years
- Disability groups research the physical accessibility of large organisations based in the area and analyse barriers to participation on local committees.

Course-based training

• Black groups jointly share their experience of oppression in their lives

• As part of a community work training course, assumptions and expectations in relation to the employment of women are examined (FCWTG 1994).

Developing critical awareness in these ways can feed into and be a part of all the variety of forms of training described earlier. Encouraging such critical debate and feedback is important for the development of a healthy and independent community sector. This leads on to a second key theme related to training as a part of community development and regeneration.

Equality

Many groups of people in the community experience discrimination, that is the process of being regularly put down by others, being subjected to negative stereotypes and being denied equal access to resources and jobs. Unless care is taken in how capacity building is set up and organised, training can be one such resource (Fuchs 1989). In fact, increased levels of employability and empowerment may be experienced primarily by articulate, already dominant groups – unless equal opportunities principles also underlie the capacity building programme.

Regeneration agencies can address this by considering and acting on questions such as:

• Does the selection criteria for the funding of capacity building include equal opportunities?

• Do area-based training needs analyses specifically look at training needs and participation levels of less mobile, less articulate groups?

• Do evaluations of capacity building provision commissioned by regeneration agencies, for example, specifically examine gender issues?

This means regeneration agencies will often need to be pro-active in implementing equal opportunities in capacity building programmes. Being mainly reactive runs the risk of primarily responding to requests which may originate from well-established groups, or only from white groups. If so, the regeneration agency may need to engage in outreach work to involve groups who may not otherwise participate in the use of training resources on an equal basis.

Equally, providing some courses that are open only to certain groups such as women or elderly people can be a useful way to target resources and redress imbalances. This may also signal to such groups that they will get a supportive reception and that the training will be suitable for them, providing an atmosphere where they can feel safe and comfortable. This form of positive action is often needed for people whose experience of discrimination has lowered their self-confidence (Griffiths 1994). Different forms of positive action in capacity building will be useful depending on needs. For example, a brief study on blocks to the participation of women in community-based training (Murphy 1994) has indicated the following in order of priority:

- lack of proper information on courses and discouraging careers advice
- attitudes of teachers and tutors in the past
- lack of child care provision
- concerns about working in a mixed group
- negative associations with school and college environments.

'*What is the nature of the context within which the capacity building takes place? The external environment is not neutral – the main issue is not just about developing new skills. Given the context of power and structural social injustice, the role of communities in society needs to be examined.*'
Senior manager, national voluntary organisation.

Many women's groups and women community workers are now actively challenging these types of blocks, both through awareness raising activities and through working on new practices in organisations and institutions (FCWTG 1994).

Planning for the provision of capacity building needs to consider perspectives based on gender, race, sexuality, disability and other forms of identity associated with discrimination; we cannot assume that community development will benefit everyone equally within the community because of existing differences in the level of access to power and resources (Williams, Seed and Mwau 1994).

Development projects in Third World countries have useful experiences to share in terms of capacity building schemes that challenge discrimination and specifically look at the wider social context within which the projects are based. Here are two examples:

- In the Beka'a valley in the Lebanon, the Aarsal Rural Development Association started as an all-male farming collective in 1985. The Beka'a valley is a poor rural area where women play an active role in family farming and animal-raising. Education is traditionally not prioritised for girls, whose labour is needed for activities associated with the home. However, a high degree of political awareness in the area, partly linked to labour union politics, has provided a framework within which ideas of gender equality have become acceptable. ARDA did not initially see a need to specifically involve women, but a consultation process led to new training courses and new forms of networking involving travel to neighbouring towns. For some of the women, this was the first time they had been outside their home town. 'The Association now recognises that women must be fully integrated at all levels of the association, including participation in planning its activities. This will make the project sustainable in achieving greater equity in gender power relations' (Oxfam 1996).

We cannot assume that community development will benefit everyone equally within the community because of existing differences in the level of access to power and resources.

- In East Africa, between 1988 and 1995, Oxfam worked with displaced people and pastoralists affected by war and insurgency in Kenya, Tanzania and Uganda. In most cases Oxfam distributed its aid – seeds, tools and household items – directly to women recognising women's authority over food and household management. In terms of capacity building, it also consciously involved women in distribution committees and actively recruited women as monitors to ensure a gender balance between monitors. 'In a context of rapidly changing social norms, it is clear that for men, seeing women take responsibility in the community makes a powerful impact and taking such action offers women the potential to develop their own organising skills' (Oxfam 1996).

Equality and training checklist

The following are examples of issues to consider, providing an initial checklist for practitioners and organisers of training.

Training needs reviews
Do these look at the needs of minority groups? Are these organised in a way that will get a response from minority groups?

Training courses
Do training courses have publicity that can attract minority ethnic participants? Are they held in venues that are accessible to people using wheelchairs? Is there crèche provision for parents? Do the materials used for content draw on the experiences of black people?

Do role plays in exercises merely maintain stereotypes of men and women? Are handouts available in large print size for participants with visual disabilities?

Group-based training
What are the criteria for choosing which groups are worked with? Can the trainer act as a role model for the group, ie. be of the same gender and cultural background as the group's members? Do the sessions fit in with the school timetable for parents?

Action-based learning
Are activities chosen for reflection and analysis ones which will raise issues on equal opportunities? Does the training help to challenge to reinforce power relations in the group?

Visits
Do visits include less confident group members? Do transport arrangements cater for elderly people? Do men take the lead roles in representing the organisation? Is the hosts' building accessible for people who have visual disabilities? Is there a loop system available?

Placements and secondments
Do placements and secondments encourage the participation of women? Are women in placements or secondments supported when experiencing sexism?

Mentoring
Does mentoring involve black people, gay people and elderly people as mentors? Are mentors chosen to also act as positive role models?

Evaluation and monitoring
Does the monitoring of participation in training consider the representation of minority groups? Do outcomes and targets consider equality issues? Does the evaluation consider the experience of participants in terms of the appropriateness of examples used in the training in relating to their own cultural backgrounds?

'The question as to whether there is a need for separate support for black community organisations was emphatically answered positively.'
The Oxford Conference

Case study:
Capacity building with refugees

This case study is based on a workshop run by Refugee Action at the Oxford conference in September 1995. It describes particular difficulties associated with capacity building work with refugees as well as exploring stages of involvement.

Refugee Action gives skilled advice to refugees and asylum-seekers from reception to resettlement, locally and nationally. It works with refugees from Bosnia, Chile, Iran, Kurdistan, Sudan, Somalia, Vietnam and many other countries, 'building community' by responding to needs, by working and learning together and by influencing national refugee policy. Refugee Action's approach to capacity building with refugees is one that:

- Emphasises sharing of existing skills, rather than the disempowering approach of ignoring existing skills and strengths

- Uses a listening approach so that capacity building is based on real needs expressed by refugees rather than worker's own views.

Particular difficulties in capacity building work with refugees are:

- when refugees are asylum seekers, the impermanence of their position affects level of involvement

- media perceptions that refugees are bogus, needy or dependent, help to create a climate of distrust and prejudice in the host population

- many refugees have a lack of historical links with host culture

- leadership may be based on traditional roles and position, for example elders rather than more democratic representation

- some refugee groups have a high turnover of active members making consistency and skill development harder.

Stages in capacity building work identified from experience with refugees are:

- Initial intensive work, for example clarifying what the group wants to achieve and helping them to develop the skills needed to do so

- Building the organisation and its links with local agencies – providing informatioon charity law, management etc.

- Low-level maintenance work as group becomes more established with occasional crisis intervention as necessary.

For more information contact: Refugee Action, telephone: 0117 942 4613.

Case Study:
Manor Training and Resource Centre, Sheffield

Manor Training and Resource Centre (MaTReC) was established on the Manor estate in April 1987, with the aim of providing local people with opportunities to obtain skills and vocational qualifications. The most distinctive feature of MaTReC is that it is owned and run by local people; the management committee consists of representatives from local community organisations and course participants. Local empowerment has been a key principle in how the centre is organised and run.

The Manor estate in Sheffield lies four miles from the city centre and consists mostly of post-war local authority housing stock. In the late 1980s the estate had a poor reputation, with high levels of unemployment and a low level of new, locally-based businesses. 'We knew that it had to be a training and education provision which could seriously address the issues of local alienation and disillusionment. It had, in other words, to be a serious and well thought out alternative to mainstream forms of provision – the *Manor Initiative* report.

So, what were the features of MaTReC's response?

- *The development of a locally-owned and locally-controlled training centre.* The building, bought with Urban Programme resources, is owned by MaTReC which is a registered charity. The centre as a training venue operates as an 'external institution' in partnership with Sheffield College. In other words, it is a 'bottom up' approach to training provision rather than the centre being run and controlled by an external agency

- *The development of a local employment policy.* This has been firstly within MaTReC itself. For example, since 1987 they have employed over 100 people in a variety of capacities, 80 per cent of whom are from the local area. Local people are involved both as administrative staff and through a tutor training programme as part of the teaching staff. Consequently many of the tutors are former course participants. This policy is important as: 'the only real way of overcoming the alienation that local people feel towards education and training is by presenting it in a familiar, non-intimidating light.' MaTReC is now involved in promoting the concept of a local employment policy with other community organisations and with local commercial employers

- *The development of course-based placements and work experience,* both in MaTReC and in estate-based community and voluntary organisations. This arrangement applies particularly in training areas such as the RSA and NVQs in information technology and business administration. Again this link not only provides a free support service to local groups, but also means participants can relate more easily to their placements than perhaps a highly-formal, large commercial organisation

- *The development of a community resource centre.* MaTReC's link between estate regeneration and training is also shown in the way the Community Resource Unit is organised. It is staffed by NVQ trainees and carries out administrative work free of charge for local community groups and organisations: 'In this way, adults work towards national qualifications in the process of helping to improve the standing and efficiency of the various groups that play an active part in the community's life.'

MaTReC also aims to increase its access to training by local people through more widely-known practices such as child care provision and learner support. Funding for the centre's programmes come from ESF, FEFC and the local authority. MaTReC is currently setting up courses specifically on community development skills, such as the RSA Advanced Diploma in the management of community groups. It is also exploring links between tailor-made provision and newly developing community enterprises on the estate.

For more information contact: MaTReC, telephone: 0114 2642194.

Practical guidelines: identifying training needs

These practical guidelines can help community practitioners to effectively identify the training needs of community organisations. Over the next 16 pages, we provide a variety of practical methods involving both direct work with groups and area-based surveys. This information is provided for you to adapt and adopt as required depending on what is most appropriate for community organisations in your regeneration area.

We are including this section because there is a lack of available practical methods which are tried and tested with the community sector. Too often there is only a partial and unsystematic attempt at identifying training needs, or methods used that are not sensitive to the needs of small-scale grassroots organisations.

These guidelines cover:

• approaches to identifying training needs
• introductory exercises
• methods for analysing training needs
• tools for assessing managerial effectiveness
• area-based surveys.

Introduction

All the methods described in these practical guidelines are participative, in particular those involving direct work with committees and groups. We consequently request that you do not use these methods unless you already have some experience in working with and facilitating groups, because their use in a participative manner requires a certain level of skill. If you do not already have this background experience, we request you to co-work with a more experienced person. This could be, for example, a trainer, consultant, community development worker or group worker. Publications that can assist in the development of this skill area are listed later.

In identifying training needs, remember you may touch on fears in group members about their own perceived inadequacies or lack of skills. This will need to be handled with some sensitivity and good listening skills. This process is helped if:

• You already have a supportive relationship with the group
• You use an approach of building from existing strengths, recognising and valuing the experience and skills people already have
• You state clearly that the overall the aim is to help people do an even better job than they are already doing.

What is especially important in identifying training needs in community organisations is that members are fully involved in the process. This is in contrast to the approach used sometimes in large public or commercial organisations, where employees' training needs may be analysed with little or no consultation.

Active involvement is important for a variety of reasons:

- In terms of community development principles, active involvement is essential for members to have control over the process

- Research on learning shows the importance of individual motivation as crucial for success. If members feel training has been imposed on them, it will produce negative responses (Cole 1993)

- In particular, remember most members of community groups are in effect unpaid volunteers and may withdraw their time and energy in this area if they feel they have not been consulted and involved. There is further discussion of this issue at the end of this section.

Approaches

In the next section we describe a variety of *practical methods* to use with groups when identifying training needs. However before we come to this, we introduce four different *approaches* to identifying training needs that have all been tried and tested with community organisations. Each approach looks at training needs from a different aspect of the activities in which the organisation is involved and may influence the choice of method. In practice, irrespective of the actual approach you adopt, you may end up with the same end result in terms of needs identified! However it is useful to have a range of different approaches available so that you use terms to which people can relate and respond, in terms of their current concerns. Here are the four approaches:

Plans

Training needs are explored in relation to the future plans of the organisation. This may be a plan to employ staff, start a new project, form a partnership with the local authority or start trading to generate income. Obviously to clarify training needs effectively such a plan needs to be in writing and in a form that group members can relate to and believe in. Assuming there is a clearly laid out written plan, this approach could involve:

- Exploring more fully how the group actually is going to get there

- Breaking down the new directions into tasks. For practical methods on this see 'Defining tasks' on page 53.

The advantage of starting from plans is that it can be a positive and forward-looking way of approaching training needs. The disadvantage is that for a less experienced group it may seem rather distant and long term compared with starting with the here and now.

Problems

Starting from problems can be a much more down-to-earth and accessible approach, especially because everyone likes to talk about their prob-

lems! The focus of this approach is on areas of difficulty or concerns the group are facing in their activities. Bringing these difficulties out may require several group sessions, carefully facilitated so as to encourage people to speak openly without damaging relationships.

The main disadvantages of this approach is that used on its own it may focus too exclusively on individual needs and current needs, rather than future needs and the needs of the organisation. Remember also the solution to some problems may not lie in training.

Tasks

Identifying tasks within the activities and roles in the organisation is a useful and widely-used approach to identifying training needs. It can be used to look both at present activities and roles, as well as future ones associated with development plans. Roles such as chairperson can be broken down into tasks and each task separated into knowledge, skills and attitudes; this is described more fully later under 'Practical methods'.

The main reservation with this approach is to avoid overwhelming people with too much detail and in particular, presenting it in a way that implies that they are currently not doing a very good job. It is important in this process to start from strengths and value people's current contribution. As new activities and roles may arise out of problem-solving and plan-based approaches to identifying training needs, task reviews often follow from these, as well as being a useful approach in their own right.

Issues

A community organisation may want to make its centre more accessible to all sections of the local community and by developing a policy and practical proposals, can then look at the related training needs. In some ways this approach is similar to the first two described above, but problems and plans may be the more formed versions arising out of an issue. Issues can and should arise in the day-to-day activities of community organisations and often reflect debates about values.

An example of how an issue can lead to identifying training needs is: a group member brings to the committee a concern about the amount of paper being wasted in the building. This leads to an open meeting being organised by the committee, to review how the centre can become 'greener' in its activities. In turn this leads to a series of workshops on environmental practice. For practical methods on this, see the later section.

Issues are a useful approach to identifying training needs because the issues may be those arising from the needs or concerns of the neighbourhood, rather than the organisation's or group members' own needs. Equally they may be issues raised through links with other community organisations and through strategies for the area developed by a local regeneration agency. This means the issue approach to identifying training needs is often a valuable link between a community organisation and the networks in which it is based.

Practical methods

This section covers practical methods for identifying training needs in community organisations. The practical methods that we now describe are divided into two broad categories:

- Methods involving direct contact and work with members of community organisations – the management committee, key organisers, key volunteers, and so on.

- Methods that involve indirect contact with a number of community organisations through an area-based survey.

Either of these categories can be combined with open meetings, workshops for a number of groups together, and so on. Another issue in examining these methods is: to what extent is the emphasis on identifying individual training needs as opposed to the training needs of the organisation itself? In practice there is often no clear dividing line between these two areas and the methods described here cater for this continuum. Some practical methods naturally correspond to certain approaches as just described, while others are adaptable to a variety of approaches.

Working with groups: Introductory exercises

The exercises described here are mostly for work with one group at a time, but could be adapted to work with a number of groups together. We start with two basic introductory exercises that are useful to use with a group which is at an early stage of understanding the need for training or its potential. These are **Levels of needs** and **Brainstorming**.

Levels of needs

Introduce the idea that in community organisations there are at least three levels of needs for training, arising from three different sets of demands:

- *Demands arising from the organisation*, such as a new business plan

- *Demands arising from jobs or roles* within the organisation, such as the role of chairperson or the job of producing publicity

- *Demands arising from relationships* with other organisations and networks, such as a new area-based regeneration plan or funding requirement.

Ask members to form three groups, and ask each group to prepare examples of one level of training needs, based on their own direct experience in their community organisation over the last year. Give each group pens and flip chart paper for feedback and allow about 20 minutes for this exercise.

Feedback may produce points such as:

Jobs/roles
- Chairperson: chairing skills, planning meetings, team building
- Treasurer: book keeping, preparing financial reports
- Committee member: being assertive, understanding responsibilities.

Organisation
- Anti-discriminatory practice
- Building management skills
- Planning skills in finance and funding
- Knowledge of charity law
- Staff management skills.

Networks/area
- Liaison and feedback skills with other groups
- Knowledge of area regeneration plans
- Communication of organisations' aims and progress to people in the area
- Ability to form partnerships for specific projects.

This exercise is fairly basic and is in no way a systematic attempt to identify needs, but it is a useful way in which to explore the issues. Inevitably there will be some overlap between the levels; at this stage it is best not to get caught up with divisions and definitions, but to encourage exploration, and an airing of views. There are ways of defining levels other than the three methods used here, and these are discussed at the end of this section.

Brainstorming

A second short exercise is to brainstorm with the whole group ways of identifying training needs. This is useful to:

- Introduce group members to the idea of identifying such needs
- Involve the group in planning how to do identify needs.

Information on how to run a brainstorming session is given in other publications on training methods (for example, Skinner 1992). The brainstorm can be started with the question 'What methods could community groups use to find out about their training needs?'

Again the aim at this stage is to get people talking and thinking about training – which they may have little experience of – rather than to produce systematic or tightly-defined lists of methods. Ideas that may come up are:

- A questionnaire for all group members to fill in
- One-to-one review/interview with each group member
- Problem-solving group sessions with the whole group
- A planning session that then looks at the training needs arising from it
- Analyse progress on targets and see if the gaps are skill-related
- Ask an outsider to observe meetings
- Examine skills needed for each formal role in the organisation, for example chair then look to see if these exist
- Have a crisis
- Unpack the new computer …

Some of these light-hearted ideas – 'have a crisis', 'unpack the new computer' – are actually very useful points to discuss the difference between training that is reactive, as opposed to that based on a conscious and careful assessment of needs.

This list is also a useful introduction to a range of methods available for assessing training needs with community organisations, which we now go on to describe.

A key point underlying the methods used in the two exercises described so far is that identifying training needs is most effective when carried out in a shared way between the community organisation and the community development worker.

Working with groups: Analysing training needs

So far we have described exercises that only really serve to introduce the theme of training needs and how these might be clarified. We now move on to explore practical methods that assist directly in assessing training needs. These come both from the fields of personnel management and community work and are called **Stocktaking**, **Future snapshot** and **Defining tasks**. We then move on to more specialist methods concerned with assessing managerial effectiveness.

Stocktaking

The stocktaking method is based on asking group members a number of questions, working for the most part in pairs, with feedback to the whole group as appropriate.

To start, after an appropriate introduction, ask people to get into pairs and to look at some or all of these questions:

• *What strengths and skills do you bring to this group?*

Remember to explain that this can be 'hard' skills such as publicity, word processing or chairing, or 'soft' skills such as team work, having an encouraging manner, and so on. Strengths can include commitment, energy, time, local information, contacts and so on. While some of these may not be directly relevant to training needs, it is useful in practice to broaden the question in this way so as to appreciate people's contribution, and to avoid alienating those whose confidence may be low.

• *Regarding your involvement with the work of this group, in what situations or with what tasks over the last year did you feel at a loss or unconfident about your skills or knowledge?*

• *What new areas of knowledge or skill do you think would have made a difference?*

It helps to give an example to illustrate this. It may have been chairing a meeting or meeting a funder. Ask people in their pairs to help each other think back over the year and jot down notes.

Working through these questions in pairs may take from 30 to 60 minutes. When asking for feedback, it is worth asking everyone to be supportive

with each other, so that people feel more able to talk openly about gaps in their skills and knowledge. If there is enough trust in the group, feedback from each pair could be charted on flip chart paper; if not, the facilitator can just report back verbally, based on what participants feel safe with. It can also be quite a relief for individuals to see that others have struggled with particular tasks. Common themes and priorities can be drawn out. A possible next step is to use the **future snapshot** method.

Future snapshot

The future snapshot method involves looking ahead to a particular point in the group's future based on its existing plans. It involves defining the group's activities and the relationships likely to be present at that future point, then devising training needs in relation to these. Existing plans consequently need to be reasonably concrete and tangible before the snapshot exercise can be carried out. The key issue is that future activities and relationships can be identified and listed as likely to be occurring at a set point in the future.

The snapshot method involves these stages:

- Before the session prepare one or two flip charts with a summary of the group's agreed action plan or business plan, in the form of a number of points
- Brainstorm with the group a list of activities and then relationships associated with the points, charting these up on flip chart paper
- Then take each activity in turn and break it down appropriately into a set of tasks
- For each task, brainstorm the main skills, abilities and broad areas of knowledge required
- For each main relationship, directly brainstorm abilities, skills and areas of knowledge required.

This process will take between one and two hours and can be quite exhausting! Some of it will be common sense and very obvious; other points and ideas produced can be perceptive and very useful.

Inevitably this exercise will produce only a broad outline of skills, abilities and knowledge, probably at most no more than half of the picture. However, the key advantage of this approach is that it aids an understanding of what will be needed, and a sense of ownership in defining training needs. The relationship aspect of this method is especially useful to focus on future possible participation in consultations and partnerships.

The next steps will be for you and the group to:

- Word process the notes from each flip chart sheet
- Expand the definition of skills, abilities and knowledge for each task and relationship using appropriate literature and the experience of others already involved in such tasks and relationships
- Design a questionnaire based on this list
- Ask individual group members to complete the questionnaire

- The combined results from the completed questionnaire can be fed back and shared with the group, to identify gaps and needs.

Obviously, let the group know about this proposed series of stages in advance and get their approval and involvement as appropriate.

Defining tasks

Defining tasks is a method of assessing training needs widely used in large public and commercial organisations (usually called job or task analysis – not a very user-friendly term!). The version described here is simplified and adapted to the setting of community organisations.

The methods described so far relate to the current or future training needs of a group of people. In contrast, defining tasks explores the training needs of one member of the group in relation to a specific task or set of tasks they have volunteered to take on. For example, a new committee member may have offered to become publicity officer but feels they will need help with this new role. Task analysis is one way to look at to and begin to define the member's training needs.

The method

The method involves four main stages. It is strongly recommended that the key participant is consulted and involved at all stages and has requested help, rather than having it imposed. The stages described here continue the example of publicity officer.

Stage 1

Working jointly with the participant, draw up a job description for the role of publicity officer. This could take the form of a list of all the tasks in which a publicity officer in a community organisation is typically involved. Ideas and resources could be obtained by:

- asking the participant for ideas

- looking at job descriptions for paid posts in the field of publicity to get ideas (but remember this 'job' is voluntary, not a paid role)

- asking the participant to visit another community group and 'shadowing' a publicity officer during their work

- looking at books on publicity for community organisations

- asking the group, based on their past experience and the snapshot exercise.

Stage 2

Devise a 'personal specification' based on the tasks described in the job description. This could contain a description of required manual and social skills, and areas of knowledge and understanding. You may not to do this for all the tasks potentially involved but only for key or central tasks, based on the main objectives of the publicity officer's role.

Stage 3

Talk through the list of personal specifications with the participant, combining their own perception of their skill and experience with your own, based on observation. This process will help to identify particular

gaps between what is needed and what the participant has already in terms of relevant skills, knowledge and experience.

Stage 4

Draw up a training action plan based on the gaps identified. See later for ideas on how to do this.

In using this method some key points to consider are:

- This can be a thorough process, but consequently may easily alienate the participant. It is important not to place too much pressure on them, especially given that their involvement in the organisation is on a voluntary basis.

- For this reason, it is recommended that this method is used only when the participant appears reasonably confident, and you are sure that they will not be overwhelmed by the process.

- The 'job' may never have been defined before in the group and the process of defining it may raise questions about the boundaries of the role. Does the publicity officer act as 'spokesperson' or is this task carried out by the chairperson? Clarifying such issues can be a useful process.

Assessing managerial effectiveness

Various forms of assessment have been devised and used as a tool for voluntary and community organisations, to assess their areas of managerial strength and weakness and to develop an action plan which helps the organisation to become more effective. As discussed earlier in the identification of training needs there is a continuum between individual training needs and organisational training needs. These next methods are located at the latter end of the continuum.

Here, we describe three different methods:

- *Organisational Health Checks.* In Nottingham, the Council for Voluntary Service has developed a 'Health check of management arrangements for voluntary organisations'. It takes the form of a questionnaire pack divided into four sections: managing the service, managing people, managing finance and managing information. Completing the form leads both to a priority rating for each section, as well as an action plan. The form is to be completed through consultation with the management committee as well as staff and volunteers; it can be completed either with or without the assistance of an external facilitator. The 'health check' is based on key points from Investors in People and can be linked to an award for individuals in management through the Open College, at Level 3. The 'health check' method was also developed further in Rotherham.

Copies of the pack can be obtained from Nottingham CVS price £5 incl. p&p. Telephone: 0115 9476714.

- *The Management NVQ.* In North Yorkshire, the Management NVQ is being effectively used as a basis for training needs analysis with community and voluntary organisations. This is a TEC-funded initiative run

by the York and North Yorkshire Training Advisory Group, which can offer a free consultancy service to assist projects to introduce NVQs. Since the Management NVQ requires the participant to be competent in certain practices and procedures, this requirement, with the involvement of the management committee, can itself facilitate a review of managerial effectiveness and corresponding training needs.

For more information contact: York CVS, telephone: 01904 621133.

- *The Hackney Standard.* In Hackney, as part of the Community Training Programme, a locally-designed set of performance measures was developed across the whole range of management disciplines. It aims to enable voluntary and community organisations to demonstrate that they are running professional organisations which can deliver quality services in an efficient and cost-effective way. The Hackney Quality Standard was devised after a review of national schemes like BS5750, Investors in People and the Management Charter Initiative, but it is tailored specifically for voluntary organisations rather than businesses. The Civic Trust now runs the Community Training Programme using the Hackney Standard to carry out comprehensive training needs analyses with participating organisations.

For more information on the Hackney Standard and the Hackney Community Training Programme contact: the Civic Trust, telephone: 0171-930 0914.

Some key points about managerial performance assessments are:

- As an approach to identifying training needs, these methods are useful precisely because they relate the organisation's practices and procedures to externally-derived standards

- Consequently, the training needs are identified in relation to organisational functioning rather than the skill development of any one individual *per se*. This is demonstrated particularly in the case of the Hackney Standard, where participation on the course can be spread between two or three representatives from each organisation

- The emphasis of these approaches is usually on the management of service delivery. It may not be appropriate for some community organisations who do not wish to provide services. It would be especially inappropriate, for example, for very small, new or unstructured groups.

Area-based surveys

So far we have examined practical methods primarily used for identifying training needs when actively working with only one community group at a time. This is a valuable approach, allowing enough detailed work to be carried out with a group. Working directly with one group is especially important for groups who are new to training and who may become participants in group-based training. Equally useful is the method of identifying training needs simultaneously with a number of community groups and organisations through area-based surveys.

Postal questionnaires are a way of reaching a large number of people. They can be used either comprehensively – sent to all known community and voluntary organisations in an area, or selectively – targeting, for

example, all disability groups. They can be used in combination with other methods, such as open meetings or workshops, to collect additional information. The case study on identifying training needs in the Batley City Challenge area gives an example of this.

A few useful practical points about using questionnaires are:

- Always include a covering letter describing how the information will be used
- Always give a clearly stated deadline for the return of the form
- Don't make the form too long or difficult to fill in
- Keep your questions clear, avoid jargon or explain terms
- Carry out a pilot run to check for clarity in advance of the main mail-out.

Content

Here is a list of issues and skill areas that can be adapted for your questionnaire form. We list here a wide range, though any one survey may not need to include all these issues:

Publicity: Leaflets, newsletters, posters etc.
Marketing: Promoting your organisation
Attracting and keeping members
Presentation skills
Budgeting, costings, cashflow forecasting
Office management/administration
Role and responsibilities of management committees
Interviewing techniques
Computer skills:
- word processing
- data bases
- spreadsheets
- desk top publishing
Writing: reports, letters, etc.
Communicating and listening skills
Staff appraisal schemes
Management team building
Decision making
Managing meetings
Assertiveness skills
Fundraising:
- approaching funders
- approaching business
Obtaining charity status
Employment law and practice
Planning for the end of the regeneration programme
Investors in People
Target setting/forward planning
Leadership skills
Customer care
Working with other organisations
Effective consultations

Using the media
Attracting users
Lobbying and campaigning
Book-keeping/accounts
Business plans/forward planning
Time management
Legal considerations of management
Recruitment/selection
Training skills and techniques
Staff supervision and support
Motivating staff
Problem solving
Conflict resolution
Group work skills
Counselling
Working with your local authority
Competitive tendering and contracts
Secondments and placements
Project appraisal and evaluation
Equal opportunities and Cultural awa
Delegation
Quality assurance systems
Working in partnerships
Effective community representation

This training needs survey list is based on an original developed by the Voluntary Sector Training Unit, Middlesbrough.

One way to make such a training needs survey form particularly effective is to include a grid with boxes against each question, to indicate which people in the organisation need the training. This could be, for example, management committee, paid staff or volunteers. However if extended in this way it would be helpful if the committee member, staff member or volunteer in question themselves completed a photocopy of the form.

Other useful questions to ask are:

- What from this list are the three most important areas of training?

- Are there any issues/skills not listed that you feel are needed in your organisation?

- What is your preferred method of training – courses, workbooks, videos, discussions, reviewing group learning from action, practical experience?

- Would you be interested in receiving one-to-one support and advice from an experienced person from a larger community or voluntary organisation (community mentoring)?

- Would you be interested in joining a learning group where members from a variety of community organisations join together to share and learn new skills?

- Would you be interested in a 'placement' with a larger community or voluntary organisation to learn new skills?

Sample Questionaire
*Here is a checklist of questions that could be included on the questionnaire
form specifically looking at what will encourage and discourage participants;
they are reprinted here from the Batley City Challenge training needs survey form.*

Please tick which of the following are most likely to encourage you to become involved in training and support sessions. Tick no more than six.

		TICK HERE
1	Topics which are relevant to me	
2	Topics which are relevant to the group	
3	Informal atmosphere	
4	Formal atmosphere	
5	Venue located in my neighbourhood	
6	Venue located in the centre of the town	
7	Daytime sessions	
8	Evening sessions	
9	Weekend sessions	
10	Comfortable venue	
11	Child care – for younger children	
12	Child care – for older children	

13	Access to transport	
14	Car parking	
15	Good publicity	
16	Good description of session content	
17	Sessions specially put on for my organisation	
18	Sessions involving other organisations	
19	Practical sessions	
20	Theoretical sessions	
21	Access for people with disabilities	
22	Sessions in languages other than English	
23	Please specify language	
24	Level of commitment required to the course by participants is clear at start	

Is there anything not on the list which would encourage you to attend?

Finally, we would like you to indicate which of the following would most discourage you from attending training or support sessions.
Please tick no more than four.

1	Not enough information about content of sessions	
2	Daytime sessions	
3	Evening sessions	
4	Weekend sessions	
5	Length of session – over 1 hour	
6	Length of session – over 2 hours	
7	Length of session – all day	
8	Charges for sessions	
9	Lack of child care provision	
10	Lack of transport	
11	Number of sessions to be attended	

Are there other things that would discourage you
from attending training or support sessions?

Thank you for taking the time to complete the questionnaire.

Questions on access and participation

A key issue in community-based training is that some people may want to participate but are in effect discouraged from attending because of the way the training is organised.

Overall, questionnaire forms are a useful method of collecting information from a large number of voluntary and community organisations on training needs. In using them bear in mind the following points:

- The response rate to a postal questionnaire is often quite low. It can be increased if there is a clear indication of the likely outcome from the form being completed and returned

- It will be useful to know who actually completes the form and their position in the organisation – this could be an initial question. Especially for forms that attempt to gather information on the needs of staff, volunteers and management committee, it needs to be indicated if such groups were actually consulted

- Beware of a bias of representation in the replies you receive. Are disability or elderly groups, for example, represented in the same proportion as on the target mailing list?

Discussion: balancing needs

A key issue in identifying training needs is – whose needs are being addressed? Is it the needs of the individual group member or the needs of the organisation? In addition, is any consideration given to needs arising from the environment within which the group is operating? This is an important issue to explore because in community-based training, the group's needs are often given exclusive priority and yet to be fully effective, all three sources of training needs should be considered:

- *Individual:* based on the methods described such as **stocktaking**, group members identify their own perceived individual learning needs

- *Organisational:* based on methods such as **future snap shot** and **defining tasks**, needs are identified, for example, in relation to roles and future plans. Based on methods such as the **organisational health check**, needs are identified, for example, in relation to achieving certain managerial performance standards

- *Environmental:* needs are identified arising from the environment within which community groups are operating. For example, from funders, a request for business plans and new forms of financial reporting; from networks, new skills for delegates to be active members. There are also needs arising from changes in legislation, for example on employment law and the responsibilities of charities. Methods described such as the **organisational health check** and **area needs survey** may cater for some of these areas.

We are not suggesting here that the methods described fall neatly into different categories, depending on the source of the training need; in practice there will be some overlap and the methods could be adapted to identify needs arising from different sources. Our main point is that if only one source is considered – arising from individual learning needs

Case study:
Batley City Challenge

This case study describes an area-based training needs analysis. In 1994, the Community Development Foundation carried out a survey of training needs in the Batley City Challenge area, West Yorkshire. In this case study, we describe the methods used, conclusions reached and practice points arising from the work. The aim of the survey project was to 'identify the training and development needs of individuals, groups and organisations involved in, or wishing to be involved in, social and community activities in the Batley City Challenge area'. It was therefore seen as important to gather as wide a cross-section of views as possible and to apply a broad definition of 'training'.

Methods
The two CDF consultants involved in the project used five different methods to carry out the survey:

- Attending and making presentations to a number of community forums to create interest in the project

- Holding two open workshops for community group representatives to initiate discussion on needs, devise a postal questionnaire and identify blocks to participation in training

- Circulating the questionnaire to 160 individuals identified as active in the community

- Collecting information from regionally-based training and consultancy organisations to establish the extent of existing and future provision

- Producing an interim report with initial findings fed back to community representatives in a specially convened group, as well as the project's steering group. A final report was produced after this consultation period.

Forty-four questionnaires were returned representing 47 communities and voluntary organisations, the form itself having been competed by ordinary committee members, chairs and secretaries as well as paid staff. As well as asking level of interest in a variety of areas of training needs the form also requested feedback on:

- factors that would encourage involvement, and

- factors that would discourage involvement.

The feedback session was used to take these issues further and to identify 'other support needs for involvement in capacity building activities, such as child care, bilingual sessions, and women-only sessions.

Some of the key conclusions were:

- The lack of adequate information on community and voluntary activity in the area. This made identifying and involving community organisations all the more difficult at the start of the survey. It was recommended that a central and accessible database be established and maintained.

- Very few organisations in Batley had a clear idea of where they wished to be in one, two or five years' time, or had a development plan. It was therefore quite difficult for them to accurately assess what skills they needed to have in place in order to achieve their objectives. This led to the conclusion that it would be 'a mistake to simply establish a training programme using the topic areas identified, without first carrying out some intensive development work with individual community organisations, to assist them to clarify their short and long term objectives and strategy for achieving them'

- The recommendation that Batley Action (the City Challenge company) should take some early initiatives in the form of training provision, to show that it was actually responding to community groups' views. Publicity for these, it was suggested, should show that the training/support sessions were directly related to the training needs survey.

For more information: contact Batley Action, telephone: 01924 473456.

– often it will not be effective in supporting community organisations to fully achieve their aims. If training is intended to increase organisational effectiveness, then training needs must also relate to organisational goals and demands arising from the environment, as well as individual goals.

'If you don't know what you don't know, how can you learn more?'
Community worker

Working with community organisations to help them identify training needs can consequently involve exploring this balancing act. Some groups may not yet be familiar enough with training or training needs reviews to consider such wider questions about needs. Some groups may feel they simply do not want to consider organisational needs and only want to get involved in training that directly relates to their individual priorities. The decision, in each case, obviously has to lie with the group, especially since – in contrast to identifying training needs in a large organisation – the participants are all giving their time and energy on a voluntary basis. It is useful to ensure that the group has had the opportunity to make a choice in a conscious way, rather than being unaware of the other possible sources of training needs. Community practitioners have a useful role to play here, acting as facilitators to enable exploration of the issues, and encouraging group members to consciously decide where they want to draw the line.

Action plans
Whatever your approach to identifying training needs, an action plan will be useful. The plan itself can state:

- Which issues and skills were identified as the most important areas for development
- What forms of training are most appropriate
- Who will be providing the training
- How it will be organised to encourage participation and reflect equal opportunities principles
- The timetable for implementation.
- How you will evaluate the outcomes.

Action plans will need to include time and resources for the evaluation of the training programme, to assess its effectiveness. An introduction to the issues involved in evaluating capacity building is given in Part 5.

Policy recommendations

Based on points raised in Part 2, we recommend that regeneration agencies and funders recognise:

- Course-based provision is only one limited form of community-based training among a wide range of options including group work, mentoring, secondments, placements and visits
- Funding for community-based training needs to cater for and encourage training needs analyses
- A careful and systematic training needs assessment is useful because training can then be based on an informed view of gaps in skills, knowledge and abilities

- Assessments are more effective when carried out in a way that involves people rather than alienates them and gives consideration to the different cultural backgrounds of group members

- Effective training needs analyses should look at individual learning needs and organisational development needs, as well as training needs arising from demands which relate to the environment within which the group is operating

- Community-based training should be organised on the basis of the two key community development principles of empowerment and equality

- Overall, community-based training has the potential not only to increase the effectiveness of community organisations and the employability of individual participants, but also to enhance the sustainability of the regeneration programme.

Further reading

Forms of training

Brush, R. 'Developing community Credit Unions in Birmingham'. unpublished

CDF. (1996) *Into the Community: A short guide for volunteers and secondments from industry undertaking placements in local community organisations.*

Cole, G. A. (1993) *Personnel Management,* D P Publications.

Federation of Community Work Training Groups and the AMA, (1990) *Learning for Action: Community Work and Participative Training.*

Hamilton, R. (1993) *Mentoring: A practical guide to the skills of mentoring,* The Industrial Society.

McEachrane, M. Lee, S. Parish, J. and Clarke, G. (1994) *Putting it on the Agenda,* Capacity Unlimited.

Pearse, J. (1993) *At the heart of the community economy,* Gulbenkian Foundation.

Skinner, S. (1992) *Training and how not to panic: A practical guide to training skills,* CETU.

Roots and Wings. (1995) *Mentoring in the Community: Report on a Pilot.*

Empowerment and equality

Association of Community Workers, (1994) *Community Work Skills Manual.*

CETU. (1993) *Assertion and How To Train Ourselves.*

Cheung-Judge, M.-Y. and Henley, A. (1994) *Equality in Action* NCVO.

Croft, S. And Bereford, P. (1993) *Getting Involved: A Practical Manual* Open Services Project.

Eade, D. and Williams, S. (1995) *The Oxfam Handbook of Development and Relief,* vol. 1. Oxfam.

Emphasise the Positive: Guide to Positive Action for Racial Equality Community Matters.

Federation of Community Work Training Groups. (1994) *Making Changes: Women, education and training.* (1994) *Women in Community Work: Feminist/womanist perspectives.*

Fuchs, S. (1989) *Tackling Training: practical guidelines for voluntary organisations* LVSC.

Griffiths, J. (1994) *Action: Training for Women* Nottinghamshire Community Work Training Group, c/o Nottingham CVS, 33, Mansfield Road, Nottingham NG1 3FB.

Honey, P. and Mumford, A. (1986) *Using Your Learning Style* P. Honey, Ardingley House, 10, Linden Avenue, Berkshire, SL6 6HB.

Hopson, B. and Scally, M. (1981) *Lifeskills Teaching* McGraw Hill.

LEDA. (1995) *The Practical Manual for Economic Development.*

Lindenfield, G. (1989) *Super Confidence* Thorsons Publishing Group.

Oxfam (1996) *Links.*

Popple, K. (1995) *Analysing Community Work: Its Theory and Practice* Open University Press.

Rochester, C. (1989) *Reaching Out into the Community* Community Matters.

Scott, C. D. and Jaffe, D. T. (1991) *Empowerment: Building a committed workforce* Kogan Page.

Wilcox, D. (1994) *The Guide to Effective Participation*, Partnership.

Williams, S. Seed, J. and Mwau, A. (1994) *The Oxfam Gender Training Manual* Oxfam.

Part 3
Developing Organisations

Developing a community organisation is similar in some ways to building a house. You may start with a small house, then add an extension when needed. Every now and then you re-decorate or take more drastic steps of knocking down a wall or two and changing the structure.

In the same way, a small community group may over time develop into a large organisation with a committee structure; it may employ staff, become a trust and even establish a separate company for trading. As with building and altering a house, some of the work can be DIY but sometimes an outside specialist is needed. Hopefully alterations don't only happen because of the leaking roof, but also as carefully planned improvements based on a review of future needs ...

In our model of capacity building, the development of organisations is equally important to the development of individual skills.

The aims of Part 3 are:
- To give you a general introduction to the practice of organisational development
- To describe possible sources of assistance to community groups
- To give an introduction to organisational development methods
- To continue to explore the themes of empowerment and equality
- To suggest ways in which regeneration agencies can organise the provision of specialist help
- To offer practical guidelines on how to make best use of specialists.

Organisational development is both an academic discipline (Mullins 1993) and a practical approach to helping organisations grow and change; our concern in this publication is only to describe the latter. Also, we are in no way attempting to teach the skills involved in organisational development but rather to give a general introduction and practical guidelines on obtaining help, which will be useful to people and agencies working in and with community organisations who are interested in capacity building.

In order to generally introduce the activities involved in organisational development we describe the process under the headings of why, who, what and how.

Why is organisational development necessary?

Community organisations may over time have a number of reasons for needing to develop and change their organisation. Here, a variety of

examples give a typical cross-section of the range of reasons; in each case the possible nature of the help required is described in brackets.

- Committee members do not communicate well with each other because of underlying inter-personal tensions (team building)
- The chairperson is domineering in manner, often excluding committee members from decisions. This has led to alienation and loss of confidence (role clarification)
- The community organisation has done well over the last two years in raising funds to build a centre but has lost contact with its neighbourhood base (grounding, that is the process of re-establishing a community base)
- The committee wants to ensure its activities are truly open to all sections of the community (equal opportunities development)
- A group of experienced community activists are now involved in estate management and experiencing difficulties accepting their new roles (management of change)
- A community association decides to become a registered charity with a separate trading company to run its bar and catering business (legal and business planning advice)
- A community organisation forms a partnership with a local college and prepares an outline funding application to the SRB Challenge Fund, to establish a major new community-based training centre (advice and information on bid preparation; facilitation work on partnership working)
- A community organisation has been reasonably successful over the last few years but members feel they are now lacking motivation and group commitment (a review clarifying aims and objectives).

You will notice from the range of issues and activities described that:
- The term organisational development is being used here in a broad sense, rather than in the more limited way described in academic texts (Mullins 1993).
- Organisational development can be useful not just to help to solve a problem or crisis but also to address a new opportunity or make better use of resources
- The need for it can arise both from internal and external demands
- The skills and experience required to respond to such requests is very varied, through obviously any one person offering organisational development assistance will specialise in particular areas.

We now move on to explore sources of help.

Who is available to offer assistance?

Increasingly community organisations are recognising that they have developmental needs and are requesting help in a planned way, rather than waiting for the next crisis. Who then is available to give such help and what different specialisms do they offer? We now examine a variety

of sources of help, briefly exploring each in turn. Because consultants are a special case we leave them until last.

Community workers

Community workers are often highly skilled in group work and facilitation methods and conscious in their approaches to translate 'empowerment' into practice. Some community workers feel that they do not know enough about organisational structures to become involved more fully in organisational development. We argue later that community workers, with some new forms of support, can often potentially be very effective as facilitators of organisational development. Their role is also discussed more fully in Part 4.

Organisational development support worker

This type of post is a new concept and a useful alternative to engaging short-term specialists. The role could involve advising and supporting community organisations on business planning, evaluation, fund-raising, financial management and partnerships. Such posts have been established, for example in the London Voluntary Service Council. They differ from community work support roles in that they focus far more on organisational and management development.

Information workers

Most parts of Britain have intermediary organisations that service and resource the voluntary and community sector. These include organisations such as rural community councils, councils for voluntary service and charity information bureaux. Information or development workers based in these agencies can often offer high quality advice and information on a wide range of legal, financial and constitutional issues. Some are able to work on a short-term basis with particular groups offering a tailor-made service, though in many cases, because of the high level of demand, the amount of assistance to any one group is limited.

Business advisers

These may be based in a TEC or local authority economic development unit. Their use by community organisations may suffer from two main drawbacks. First, the values underlying their advice may often be drawn from the private sector, without adequate consideration of the needs and values of the community and voluntary sector. Secondly, advice-giving as a form of short term intervention can sometimes appear as an outside solution producing little real commitment or ownership from participants. Many advisers are aware of these issues and try to work in a more participative manner.

Experienced group members

There is an important case for developing facilitation and training skills among members of community organisations so that they themselves can be a useful source of assistance in organisational change. The main drawback is that the individual may be too 'close to home' to act or be seen in an objective enough way to be really effective. One way forward to solve this possible dilemma is for experienced community group members to work with other groups, rather than their own. A community

consultants skills course developed by Community Matters specifically aims to train local activists as facilitators, who are then available to work with other groups. For more information see Part 2.

Trainers

This may be a surprising inclusion, given the emphasis in Part 2 on training. However, remember as well as focusing on individual learning needs, a training programme can also be based on organisational needs and consequently may address organisational development. Examples of these are given in Part 2. In addition, a trainer working with a group may have already built up an effective working relationship which could form a solid basis for more in-depth and challenging work on organisational change, assuming they have the necessary skills and experience.

Researchers

Researchers can help indirectly with organisational development, for example by assessing the impact of a new funding arrangement or organisational structure on the work of the group at delivery level. Some researchers are increasingly committed to making their skills accessible to community organisations, for example those involved in Community Operational Research. A key issue is the ability of the individual researcher to relate to and easily communicate with community organisations.

Consultants

Consultants are increasingly being used by the voluntary and community sector, yet research described later shows many groups and organisations have little idea of what their role is and how they might be effectively used (Hyatt 1995). We now explore their activities in more detail.

In practice the work of consultants can be broken down into four roles:

The adviser

Here, the consultant provides specialist information and skills. For example, this could be fund-raising skills or information on the legal structures required to establish a development trust.

The researcher

Here, the consultant collects and analyses information on behalf of or with the group to tackle a specific task or problem. The information collected can be both quantitative and qualitative, and as part of this role the consultant may also present options for the future based on the findings.

The analyst

Here the consultant uses their knowledge of how organisations work to give an analysis of the cause and nature of the problem, or proposes a new structure for the group to be able to respond to a new funding opportunity. An analogy here is that the consultant acts like a doctor, collecting information on the group's problems and then offering a 'diagnosis'.

The facilitator

Here, the consultant's role is to enable the group to examine the nature and cause of the problem, and to use practical methods to help them collectively generate solutions.

In practice there is often no clear dividing line between these roles and all four may be used at varying points in the relationship.

Many funders, regeneration agencies, community and voluntary organisations have a knee-jerk response to organisational problems – 'bring in a consultant'.

Research funded by the Joseph Rowntree Foundation (Hyatt 1995) indicated that many of the techniques used by consultants, such as brainstorming, visualisation or developing aims and objectives, do not require specialist knowledge. In eight examples examined, the consultant's work involved varying degrees of facilitation, using skills such as listening, reflecting, clarifying and recording, to enable the group to tackle their problems themselves. This suggests that a wide range of practitioners, in particular community workers, could take on this kind of facilitation role.

Discussion

This brief review of roles usually carried out by consultants and other available sources of assistance indicates that there is potential for a wide variety of forms of specialist help available.

In practice some of these sources can provide only a very specific and limited form of assistance, such as information officers and researchers. However, our main point is that many funders, regeneration agencies, community and voluntary organisations have a knee-jerk response to organisational problems – 'bring in a consultant'.

In contrast, a more informed approach to using specialists would be to carefully consider the options available and regard the use of a consultant *per se* as only one route to follow.

In order to encourage this more informed approach and diverse view of available assistance, we recommend that the term 'specialist' is more appropriate than consultant. For example, if the problem is lack of team work, the appropriate specialist may be an experienced community worker. If the need is for an independent evaluation of a project, the appropriate specialist may be a community-oriented researcher rather than a consultant *per se*. Different specialists will obviously vary in the extent to which they work in an enabling manner; there are still cases where the experience of using a specialist has been one of disempowerment, leaving the group with few new skills or little sense of ownership of the way forward.

Organisational development cannot and should not be used as a substitute for longer-term community development support.

More fundamentally, there is the issue of the context of assistance for organisational development with community organisations. It cannot and should not be used as a substitute for longer-term community development support. Organisations may not be ready to develop further without properly resourced community development support. Also, specialist assistance is by definition short term and cannot replace ongoing community work involvement. Community work is explored in more detail in Part 4.

Having initially explored the why and who, we now move on to explore methods used in organisational development.

Checklist on equal opportunities

Equal opportunities and the principle of equality needs to be considered at every stage of involvement by specialists with community organisations. Here, we provide a checklist to support both specialists and community groups to consider these essential issues. All the quotes in this section are from feedback given at the 1995 Oxford conference, Capacity Building with Black and Ethnic Minority Groups.

- *Choice of specialists:* some discriminated groups may want to only work with a person who has similar personal experience:

  'In particular where white workers are working with black groups, there are potential issues of power and control to be addressed. Are white specialists looking at these issues?'

- *Contact:* is contact with the group by the specialist channelled and influenced by a domineering person? Does the brief reflect the concerns of everyone in the group?

- *Facilitation:* if the specialist is involved in running sessions with the group, facilitation work will need to ensure the chance for equal involvement by all participants, without one or two more vocal people dominating. Some people may need signers or translators to enable them to participate more fully.

- *Exercises and methods:* do these encourage the sharing of different cultural backgrounds and experiences? Do they encourage people's different ways of expressing themselves? Do they discriminate against people who have difficulties in reading?

- *Models of organisational development:* are these based on white cultural assumptions or dominated by male perspectives?

  'There is a broader question about whose concept is the concept of "capacity building" anyway; for example, is it about persuading community groups to organise in ways which funders and public authorities find more comfortable and convenient?'

- *Funding of the use of specialists:* funders may often need to examine their criteria of grant aid in the light of equal opportunities issues:

  'Funders need to build their capacities and shift to meet the needs of groups; the learning and adjustments should not be all one way.'

- *The availability of specialists:* is it mainly well-established or white groups that are requesting and getting help from specialists? Is there a need for a more pro-active scheme promoting the availability of specialists for minority ethnic groups?

- *The development of black support centres:* In Bristol, for example, a Race Equality Development Agency has been established offering information, training and consultancy services to support involvement of the black voluntary sector.

What methods are commonly used?

In this section we describe and explore the use of methods used by specialists in organisational development work with community groups. This review aims to help readers to be better placed, to enable community organisations to understand and benefit from organisational development. Inevitably this description of methods is only partial and introductory. Our aim is not to attempt to pass on the skills involved in these methods; it is mainly to help develop your understanding of their function.

The following brief summaries provide some examples of methods commonly used by specialists working with groups involved in organisational development and change. Some are used widely; others are less well-known. References are given for further information.

Brainstorming
Brainstorming is a well-known, often misused method of generating a large number of ideas collectively in a short space of time (Skinner 1994).

Clarifying aims and objectives
An accessible way of enabling groups to achieve a collective agreement on both long term aims and how they will achieve them (Gawlinski and Grassle 1988).

Clarifying roles
A useful method when there is confusion about individual responsibilities and areas of work. Participants share perceptions and information about their roles, with opportunities to air misunderstandings in a constructive framework (Skinner 1994).

SWOT analysis
SWOT stands for Strengths, Weaknesses, Opportunities and Threats. These four headings are surprisingly effective to help groups review their situation and begin to establish future plans (Lawrie 1994).

Portfolio analysis
A method of categorising an organisation's activities, under four headings that enable a project to adopt a balanced approach to future planning (Lawrie 1994).

The Four Steps
A simple but very effective method to help groups solve problems based on four steps or stages of exploring the ideal, the current reality, the blocks and the way forward (Skinner 1994).

Gap analysis
A reasonably straightforward method to assist in strategy formation that considers the gap between where the organisation is now and where it wants to be. Gap analysis can be applied to output targets or, for example, less specific quality issues (Barnard and Walker 1994).

How do these types of practical methods fit into the overall process of organisational development? Here is one example describing a specific piece of organisational development work in the form of a set of stages:

- Initial contact and exploratory meeting between the specialist and the group

- Agreement on roles and initial brief

- Clarification of the need or problem using research and practical methods

- Sharing and initial review of 'diagnosis'

- Exploration of solutions and new structures using practical methods

- Follow up meetings looking at implementation of solutions

- Evaluation using practical methods

- Final report and completion.

Please note that these simplified stages are not offered as a prescriptive model. As can be seen from this one example, the use of methods can occur at a number of points. In fact, the process of clarifying the need, problem or nature of the opportunity, as described later, can itself be a major part of the specialist work with a group.

So far in Part 3 we have begun to explore the why, who and the what of organisational development as an aspect of capacity building. We now move on to look at two aspects of the 'how' – how agencies can organise provision of specialist assistance, and how practitioners and groups can organise the effective use of specialists.

How can assistance be provided?

Regeneration agencies can play a major role in the provision of organisational development assistance for community groups. Here is a checklist of ideas:

'Recognition of the work of community organisations through award schemes is also an important form of assistance and support.'
Former Director, national voluntary sector organisation

☐ Organise and maintain a directory of specialists, listing advisers, consultants, information officers and so on

☐ Establish a central fund to grant aid organisations wishing to engage specialists on a paid, short term basis

☐ Establish a community chest fund that can be used to quickly provide groups with small amounts of money for help with preparing briefs and tenders. This would be prior to engaging a specialist but may itself require paid help, for example for two days

☐ Encourage provision for paying for specialist help within mainstream revenue funding to community organisations

☐ Fund intermediary organisations, such as consortiums of larger voluntary organisations, that can in turn provide a service of organisational development assistance to community groups (see the Pan-London Capacity Building Programme case study in Part 4)

☐ As an agency, directly employ specialists who can offer assistance to groups

□ As an agency, develop a training programme for potential specialists, including experienced members of community organisations

□ Establish a pool of specialists who are chosen specifically to work with community groups

□ Work in partnership with other regeneration agencies to provide funding and support for organisational development assistance

□ Establish and maintain systems to provide information to community organisations, for example on funding, charitable status, and requirements as good employers.

Case study
Bethnal Green City Challenge

This case study provides a good example of a pool for specialists created by the regeneration agency.

Bethnal Green City Challenge (BGCC) is based in a multi-racial part of East London and has established a scheme of specialist assistance for targeted community groups as one element of its capacity building strategy. Through a tendering process, BGCC has recruited a team of freelance fund-raisers. These specialists are then each matched with three or four community organisations, on the basis of:

- Organisations that are in receipt of capital programme funds from BGCC and where the agency perceives a need for them to secure funding from other sources

- Organisations that have approached BGCC directly for assistance to diversify funding streams

- Organisations identified by BGCC-employed community workers as being in need of specialist assistance.

Each organisation is offered a certain number of days' work and is matched with a proposed specialist; organisations have power of veto if they are unhappy with the match. The role of the fund-raisers, as defined by BGCC is to:

- Directly raise funds for the organisation

- Share skills through one-to-one mentoring

- Develop the organisation through direct work with the organisation's management committee.

In other words, the aims of the specialist help is clearly not only in terms of financial targets, but also to develop skills and organisations so as to create sustainable structures. This aspect of the use of specialists is seen as a crucial part of BGCC's continuation strategy.

This scheme was established consciously to provide a resource to targeted community organisations in the agency's area while saving the organisations themselves the time and demands of individually recruiting specialists.

For more information contact: Bethnal Green City Challenge,
telephone: 0171-613 3232.

Practical guidelines: how to make good use of specialists

These practical guidelines are for practitioners who are working with community organisations so that they can enable such organisations to use outside specialist assistance effectively. The guidelines will also be of interest to managers and providers of capacity building programmes so that they more fully appreciate the issues involved in organisational development.

Over the next seven pages, we provide a series of steps to go through – not all of these may apply to you and the community organisation you may be working with. In practice, the process may not include every step or necessarily be in the order given here. In particular, much of this material, such as tendering, will be inappropriate for small amounts of specialist assistance. However, we have provided a reasonably comprehensive set of guidelines to act as a framework for you to adapt and adopt as required.

Usually specialist assistance is a short-term relationship; mostly it involves payment though in some cases, the help can be free. Whether paid or not, it is important that the community organisation benefits from the relationship and the specialist is well-treated and made good use of.

This framework will help you to think about how to help groups approach and use an outside specialist; it is based on research and extensive field work with community organisations (Hyatt 1995 and Skinner 1994).

We now describe each step of the framework in turn.

Agreeing on the need for outside help

To make good use of an outside specialist, the community organisation – for example the management committee – will first have to collectively agree that help is required. In some cases specialists have discovered at a first meeting that half the committee members do not want them to be involved! Agreeing help is necessary involves two stages:

- Recognising there is a problem to solve or opportunity to take
- Accepting that outside specialist help is required to help solve the problem or to explore the opportunity.

It is important to separate out these two stages. In the first stage the group may need facilitation help in order to identify the nature of a problem or opportunity. Such initial help could be given by a community worker or a specialist working with the group on a very short-term basis, such as two days. The need for short-term help just to clarify whether a more substantial amount of organisational development assistance is required, suggests a system being established to distribute small amounts of money, for example through a community chest.

In practice, many problems can be and are rightly solved using the group's own resources; or the group has enough skill and knowledge to make full use of a new opportunity without additional help.

'Sometimes our work is wasted as the group could have done it themselves.'
Community consultant

Even when it is decided some additional form of help is needed, it may not necessarily be outside help – an experienced group member may be able to act as facilitator for an 'away day' review, or the group may already have a community worker working with them. It depends on the skills and roles needed. As mentioned earlier, there may be benefits from using someone not already part of or well-known to the group. Using an outsider who regularly works with a range of groups can have the advantages of bringing in an overview of problems experienced by the community sector.

If it is decided to seek more substantial outside assistance, the next step will be choosing a specialist.

Choosing a specialist

There are three main ways to choose a specialist:

- Through a formal process of tendering
- Through an informal process of individual recommendation
- By making use of an existing pool of specialists.

The process of tendering involves drawing up a brief for work needed, advertising through newsletters and networks and then interviewing to choose the most suitable person. In contrast, the process of recommendation involves finding out about potential help through word of mouth, based on the past experience of other organisations. In both cases the specialist can be asked to provide written evidence of their suitability.

An alternative method is where a regeneration agency or other outside funding body sets up a pool of specialists who are checked for suitability to work with the voluntary and community sector. Groups can then choose one from a set list subject to interview.

We now examine the advantages and disadvantages of each of these three methods of choosing a specialist.

Tendering

Advantages
The advertising part of the process, if carried out carefully, is a way of making the selection process fairer because it casts the net more widely.

Disadvantages
The process is demanding in terms of time, money and skills; some community organisations feel overwhelmed with the prospect of this especially if they have never done it before. The process is especially time-consuming if only short-term help is required. Also, even after a careful process of advertising and interviewing, an inappropriate person can be chosen. Because of these disadvantages tendering is not often

used by community organisations when recruiting specialists. Some area-based schemes have been established specifically to help groups with the tendering phase.

Individual recommendations

Advantages

This method is cheaper and quick to carry out compared with tendering. Recommendations from trusted contacts can be very useful.

Disadvantages

Because there is no advertising involved, this process can unfairly exclude specialists not already known in the area or in local networks. It could lay the group open to accusations of 'nepotism'. In addition, this is especially a cause for concern if in practice, the process for example reduces the number of black people or women who might otherwise have been interested in the work. Another disadvantage is that just because a specialist is effective with one particular task they may not necessarily be as effective with a different problem.

Using a pool

Advantages

Again, this method is quick to carry out compared with tendering. It has the potential advantage over individual recommendations that the specialist may have been more systematically assessed for suitability.

Disadvantages

The group's choice will be limited by the screening process that an outside organisation used to create a pool of specialists. In some cases, the regeneration agency itself chooses the individual specialist for the group, which may cause resentment and contribute to a lack of involvement.

Bearing in mind the different advantages and disadvantages, we recommend:

- A tendering process is inappropriate for relatively small pieces of work and for unpaid assistance

- When tendering is appropriate, groups may often need support and advice to help them prepare for it

- When the recommendation process is used, it should be carried out in a way that does not exclude minorities. For example, it can be carried out to specifically include a certain proportion of black people and women

- When a pool system is established, this will also need to consider equal opportunities principles.

Defining the brief

Having a brief helps to clarify the need for and the aims of the work. It can also act as a set of guidelines both for the group and specialist as the work progresses. Furthermore, it can be the basis of an evaluation towards the end of the work. If selection of the specialist is made through tendering, an initial brief is essential and is certainly useful with the recommendations and pool methods of selection.

An initial brief can be enlarged and made more specific once the person is chosen, based on a further exploration of needs, if appropriate. The amount of time spent devising a brief will depend partly on the importance of the piece of work and partly on the likely length of the whole piece of work in which the specialist will be involved. If it is only one day, then preparing the brief may need take only half an hour.

It is useful if a brief contains a description of some or all of the following:

- The aims of the work
- The nature of the need, opportunity or problem
- The likely timetable for the work
- The specialist's role and responsibilities
- The group's roles and responsibilities
- Resources available to the specialist during the work
- Arrangements for communication and management of the specialist – who they take direction from during the work
- How equal opportunities principles will be considered and acted on
- How skills will be passed on to the group during the work
- A description of the key milestones to be achieved
- The form of any report or other output if required
- The form of evaluation of the specialist's work.

'Even on small pieces of work, it's essential to have a clear brief.' Community consultant.

Many community organisations request help in preparing such a brief and community workers can have an important support role here. In practice, when not involved in the more formal process of tendering, many groups have only a half-formed brief, choose a specialist and then use the first stage of involvement with them to clarify it more fully. A degree of flexibility seems appropriate in such cases.

However, if a full tendering process is chosen, it is important that enough information is provided for potential specialists to respond, given that a short list for interview will be drawn up based on their written replies.

Checklist on briefs

Here is a useful checklist concerning preparing and agreeing on briefs. As with any checklist, not all the points will be useful for you and your situation.

☐ Ensure all participants who are likely to be involved see the final version before proceeding with the work.

☐ Check with members of minority groups within the organisation that they are satisfied with the brief.

☐ Beware the brief does not suggest the solution to the problem in hand too firmly before the work has even started!

☐ Consider if other organisations may need to be consulted about the brief if the work may require their involvement

☐ Include a statement on confidentiality as appropriate

☐ Check the brief is not written in such vague language that no-one can really understand it; or it gives the specialist too much leeway to follow their own agenda.

As you can see, the process of devising and agreeing on a brief for using a specialist is quite complicated! In particular, it may be possible to draw up a full brief reflecting the real needs of the organisation once some initial exploration has been carried out by the specialist with the group. One way forward is to have two briefs:

• An initial brief, used for selection of the specialist

• A second, full brief that then becomes the basis for the work, after the specialist carries out a further exploration of needs.

Depending on the situation, a contract based on the brief may need to be given to the specialist involving additional information on payment and accountability. More specific information on how to prepare tenders and contracts is provided in *Managing Consultancy* (Rogers, 1990).

Interviews

Whether using tendering, a pool or recommendations, it is important to interview the potential specialists before their involvement is agreed on. This applies even if the group is considering using only one person.

The following is a useful checklist of useful information to find out, either through written material provided prior to the interview or verbally:

• What is their past relevant experience, especially in terms of working with community organisations?

• What particular skills and knowledge do they have to offer for this piece of work?

• In what ways will they use their involvement to build the group's own skills and confidence?

• How will they base their work on equal opportunities principles?

• How much time will they need to do the job?

• How can a process of evaluation of their involvement be integrated into the work?

Exactly how these questions are worded and presented will vary according to the needs of the piece of work.

Clarifying the need

As just mentioned, the first step in the work will often involve the specialist finding out more about the problem, need or opportunity that prompted the request for help. The specialist may consequently be involved in a process of information gathering; this process will obviously vary widely depending on the nature of the role, as described earlier. The group itself can have a role to play in this process.

Here are some of the information gathering sources that as appropriate might be involved:

Internal sources

- Members of the group, management committee, board, etc.
- The wider membership of the organisation
- Users and past users
- Staff
- Volunteers
- Minutes of past meetings
- Existing statements on aims, vision, objectives etc.
- Annual reports, grant applications, evaluation reports

The specialist may use a mixture of reading, attending meetings, interviews and observation in collecting information. In some cases, the specialist may carry out a review of the organisation using methods such as an organisational health check, as described earlier in Part 2.

External sources

- Funding organisations
- Regeneration agencies
- Other locally-based community organisations
- Locally-based voluntary agencies
- Members of key local networks
- Community workers
- Experienced community activists
- Trainers and specialists used in the past.

External sources who have a particular interest are sometimes referred to as 'stakeholders'. In practice, only a limited number of outside sources may be used, especially as information collection is time consuming. However, this potentially wide range of sources does raise some questions for the community organisation to consider, in its contribution to assisting the information gathering process:

With internal sources:

- Is any information confidential?
- Are there any key, past incidents the specialist should be aware of?
- Is the specialist's information gathering work unintentionally excluding certain sources because of some bias? For example, does a white male specialist relate mostly to a white male chairperson and give dominance to their views?

With external sources:

- Will the source of information gathered be anonymous in terms of the individual who gives it, if it involves negative views and opinions?
- When meeting funders, how will the specialist present the group? Will it come across in a negative manner?

• Will the specialists collect information from other agencies and organisations on their own, or working jointly with group members?

Key points with either internal or external sources are:

• The group needs to be open to letting the specialist gather perhaps new and challenging information if it is required for the task

• The specialist needs to carry out their work in a way that does not take control away from the group.

This means the specialist needs to work with the group, not just for it, and engage in consultation with group members on sources of information gathering as appropriate. If the specialist is making an analysis of the problems the organisation is experiencing, then this can be presented and shared in a participative manner, rather than imposed as an 'expert' view. In these ways the specialist can base practical work on community development principles. Research has shown that in practice specialists do not always work in this way – see the case study on p.81 for further material on this.

Reviewing mid-way

Collecting information, whether internal or external, is all part of the work and can lead to, or be combined with, use of the practical methods for organisational development described earlier. These may, for example, take the form of a number of workshop-type sessions, using a variety of methods involving all group members. A useful step at the mid-way point in the process is for the group and specialist to have a review of progress to date. This is likely to form part of the evaluation of the specialist's role. Exactly what form this review takes and when will vary depending on the nature of the assistance and work.

The mid-way review can be a useful opportunity to check on certain questions and issues:

• Are the group members learning new skills from their relationship with the specialist?

• Does the specialist's work seem on track in terms of the overall aims and remaining time?

• Are there any areas of communication and support for the specialist that need clarifying?

• Is the specialist enjoying the work? If not, why not?

• Does the group feel in control of the process or that solutions or new directions are being imposed?

Once these and similar issues are clarified, the specialist can be given the go-ahead to proceed with the rest of the work. A mid-way review can be very useful to ensure good use of a specialist.

'After 12 months our specialist fund-raiser had raised nothing and taught us very little.'
Residents' association

Receiving final reports

A report is definitely not always the most effective way to complete a piece of specialist work with a community organisation. In fact, presenting a final report may be in some cases an unnecessary and even unproductive preoccupation! It can be combined with or, in some cases, substituted by:

- A final feedback and review session where key findings are presented and shared in a more accessible form
- An open day with a display showing the results of the work
- A manual or handbook sharing skills and findings
- A business plan or funding strategy rather than a more general report
- Production of a video film.

Where a report does seem appropriate, beware that:

- It takes weeks to arrive, by which time it has passed its usefulness
- The report itself is seen as the main outcome from the work, rather than any real changes occurring in the organisation
- It is produced without enough consultation with group members
- The report is relied on too heavily to solve current problems; action is delayed while awaiting for its arrival!
- The report does not provide enough detail to be useful
- It wrongly contains confidential material!

Be assertive to get what you asked for – and realistic not to expect more than was agreed on. Ask for a draft before the final version is provided – this gives you opportunities to request improvements if you think it does not come up to the required standard.

In discussing the aims of the report also consider at an early stage:

- Is this for internal use only or available to outside organisations, and funders in particular?
- If so, is it presented in a way that maintains the right image for the group?
- If not, what opportunities will there be for the group to comment or amend?

At a later stage you will need to consider:

- What action points arise from the report and who is responsible for carrying them out?
- Generally, what happens next in terms of relations with the specialist? If this is the end of your relationship, apart from feedback and evaluation, don't forget to say 'thank you'.

'After months of hard work with the group, at the end no one even said "Thank you".'
Consultant, West Yorkshire

Case study
The Holmewood Redevelopment, Bradford City Challenge

This case study of the Holmewood Central Redevelopment, Bradford, is an interesting example precisely because the work involved facilitating organisational change rather than enabling individual learning.

Holmewood is a large council estate in the City Challenge area of Bradford. Alongside a substantial programme of housing improvements, Bradford City Challenge is funding the establishment of a large scale multi-purpose leisure and community centre. The project involves both new build and major structural improvement to four adjacent existing buildings, to be the office and activity base for eight user organisations. Because the redevelopment plans involved integration of an existing collection of buildings into one new co-ordinated centre, it created an opportunity for shared use of space and facilities as well as a potential for joint user management. The eight user organisations include small voluntary projects, an already-active small training centre, a branch library and an area base for the authority's youth service. While these user organisations had the potential to co-operate and share resources, there was a long history of misunderstandings and a lack of clarity as to how the users would work together to manage the new centre.

The capacity building task
With users' approval, Bradford City Challenge invited CDF to work with the committee or representatives to develop a management structure. There was also a need to help to establish ground rules for the use of shared space, as well as generally speed up the process of agreeing on the new activities (such as the community café) and new roles (such as centre co-ordinator).

There were a number of complex questions to be tackled:

- Who would be on the new management committee? Just representatives of user organisations or would 'community representatives' be included and if so, which ones?

- Would the voluntary organisations in the building pay rent to the local authority (who owned the buildings) and if so, how much?

- How would the space allocated to any user organisation be made available for 'community use' when not being used by them? Who decides on this use and what happens to the income for room hire?

These and many other contentious issues hung over the regular and rather tedious meetings of the user representatives, who in themselves were neither constituted as an organisation nor communicating well as a group.

How then in such a setting can capacity building, focusing on organisational change, be carried out in a manner based on community development principles? Here is a brief account of work on these tasks that brings out some of these themes:

- The first step was to check quite carefully that all organisations were willing participants in the new management structure. An early visit to one project revealed a sense of coercion that needed resolving before proceeding

- A second step was to decline to become identified as 'experts' offering an 'objective' appraisal of management structure options for the centre. We felt such an approach would not enable a sense of ownership of an agreed structure and instead we proposed to adopt a clearly defined facilitation role.

- A third key step was to invite representatives of all parties involved to an open planning meeting, both to approve the facilitators' brief for CDF and to agree on a decision making system for the proposed 'away day'. The decision making system agreed on was one of consensus with majority voting as a back-up arrangement when consensus involved too much time. Participants appreciated being involved in this aspect of planning at an early stage rather than arriving at an 'away day' with a system already imposed or poorly prepared.

What happened?

In practice, there were two 'away days', carried out in spring 1995 and held in a neighbouring environment centre. Both went reasonably well with good levels of attendance and participation. By agreeing on a future composition and management function, the user representatives became a management committee. As the two days progressed, inter-personal and inter-agency tensions reduced and the new committee felt at last there was some progress on arrangements and action. A system for under-used space was established and proposals for a crèche and new café progressed substantially.

Discussion

Here was a building-based regeneration scheme, involving over £1 million of hard-won resources, requiring a sustainable management system with local involvement that would last beyond the limited years of City Challenge. In this case, the emphasis of capacity building was on organisational change to help establish a meaningful management structure, rather than assist individuals in their own skills development. In such a setting, no doubt both are often needed and a programme of training in planning and committee skills would now be useful on Holmewood. What does seem important from this example, is the need to choose carefully between an emphasis on organisational change as opposed to individual learning where the former is an initial priority.

Certainly the experience on Holmewood to date has shown appropriate capacity building support, based on community development principles, can be of some assistance to develop new and challenging management systems for a multi-purpose centre.

Case study
Using consultancy methods with community organisations

This case study reviews research carried out in 1994 by the Community Development Foundation. The research was funded by the Joseph Rowntree Foundation and looked at the effectiveness of eight external, short term (less than six months) interventions by specialists. The study points to a number of lessons for good practice that especially focus on the issue of empowerment.

The specialists used a wide variety of techniques including public meetings and questionnaires, brainstorming, problem analyses, role play and visualisation. The community organisations they worked with included three community centres, an estate management board, an environmental action group, a development association, a black community action group and a community arts centre. To assess the effectiveness of the specialists' work, CDF involved researchers who conducted interviews with group members, the specialists themselves and members of other interested organisations, such as local councils and funding bodies.

In some cases there were very tangible practical results such as the establishment of charitable status or a new financial system; in others, the group itself developed stronger skills, such as increased confidence or a clearer sense of direction. Consultancies also contributed towards more effective relationships with outside agencies and in winning grant aid.

Empowerment issues arising from the study

Agreeing the consultant's role

In the most successful cases, groups had a clear understanding of the specialist's role and responsibilities. However, in half the case studies there was no clear contract between the specialist and the community group. This gave rise to misunderstandings about whom the specialist could contact and involve in particular tasks, and to what extent the specialist was expected to do the work as opposed to enabling the group to do the work themselves. There is value in actually setting down what a community group is going to get for its investment in the consultancy.

Agreeing the aims of the consultancy

An important factor in the effectiveness of the specialist assistance was the extent to which the group was involved in setting the aims. In some groups, for example, the specialist had initially helped to diagnose problems and the consultancy therefore started with clear objectives. In others, the aims of the consultancy changed as the specialist unearthed new and different issues to deal with. These cases were also successful – largely because the group and the specialist agreed about what was generally expected and the group members were involved in setting and reviewing these aims.

Avoiding over-dependency

Specialists need to consider carefully how they can most effectively empower the group.

The examples showed that consultants need to be highly aware of roles they adopt with groups with which they are working. In one case, the consultant consistently took a lead role which encouraged over-dependence, whereas in another, the specialist consciously changed role from 'doer' to mentor, in order to facilitate the sharing of new skills with group members. The research suggests specialists need to consider carefully how they can most effectively empower the group, adapting their approaches according to needs and where possible, to adopt a shared agreement on roles.

Choosing a specialist

Evidence from the eight examples suggests involving the group in the selection of a specialist can increase the effectiveness of the whole process. However, in most of the case studies the decision to use a specialist came from an outside agent, such as a community worker, rather than from the group itself. Most of the groups studied didn't know when to bring in a specialist, or how to find or select one. In fact in all the cases, the choice of consultant was a matter of personal recommendation, rather than the result of a selection process. If specialists are to play a role in community groups, this research suggests that ways should be found of raising awareness about when to use, how to find and how to select appropriate assistance.

Further information on this research is contained in
Calling in the Specialist (Hyatt 1995).

Policy recommendations

Based on points explored in Part 3, we recommend that regeneration agencies and funders recognise:

- That organisational development is an equally-important aspect of capacity building as the development of people

- That consultants are not the only effective available resource to assist in organisational development. A range of other practitioners also have roles to contribute, and the term 'specialist' rather than 'consultant' is consequently more appropriate

- Regeneration agencies have a range of options available in the provision of specialist assistance, including the production of directories, funding use of specialists by community groups and by directly employing specialists

- In order to engage specialists themselves, community organisations may need initial support, advice and guidance; this could in some cases be provided by locally-based development workers. In other cases, initial short-term paid help may be needed, for example running an 'away day' to help clarify needs, or prepare briefs for the more substantial use of specialists. This suggests the establishment of community chests as a flexible and rapid mechanism to respond to such requests for help

- Funding the use of specialists by community organisations needs to cater for and encourage evaluation of their use

- The selection and use of specialists needs to be based on equal opportunity and community development principles

- Provision of assistance to the community sector for organisational development cannot and should be not be seen as a substitute for ongoing community development support.

Further reading

Barnard, H. and Walker, P. (1994) *Strategies for Success. A self-help guide to strategic planning for voluntary organisations*, NCVO.

Gawlinski, G. and Graessle L. (1988) *Planning Together*, NCVO.

Hope, P. (1992) *Making the Best Use of Consultants*, Framework in Print.

Hyatt, J. (1995) *Calling in the Specialist*, CDF.

Lawrie, A. (1994) *The complete guide to business and strategic planning for voluntary organisations*, Directory of Social Change.

Martin, N. and Smith, C. (1993) *Planning for the Future. An introduction to business planning for voluntary organisations*, NCVO.

Mullins, L. (1993) *Management and Organisational Behaviour*, Pitman.

Pugh, D. S. and Hickson, D. J. (1989) *Writers on Organisations*, Penguin.

Rogers, R. (1990) *Managing Consultancy*, NCVO.

Skinner, S. (1994) *Change and how to help it happen*, CETU.

Stanton, A. (1989) *Invitation to Self-Management*, DabHand Press.

Part 4
Developing Community Infrastructure

The community infrastructure is part of the environment within which community organisations operate. In practice it involves the provision of facilities and resources specifically targeted to increasing the capacity of community and voluntary sector organisations. These facilities and resources can take a variety of forms, as described below. To continue the house analogy used to describe organisational development at the beginning of Part 3, community infrastructure is the equivalent of the mains services – roads, drainage, electricity, gas, water supplies – all essential to enable the house to be lived in, maintained and developed.

Community infrastructure, as an environment for successful community-based regeneration, can take a variety of forms:

- Resources
- Networking
- Participative structures
- Community development support
- Professional capacity building.

These five forms are now discussed in turn. Part 4 does not have a separate page on policy recommendations for regeneration agencies, because the whole of this section relates to policy issues.

Resources

'I see a capacity building strategy as identifying the basic level of resources which should be available in an area to enable both existing and potential groups to organise.'
Community liaison officer

Many members of grassroots community organisations will, if asked, give you a long list of resources that their group needs to be more effective – legal information, access to printing equipment, office equipment, a photocopier and so on. However, while many community organisations are keenly aware of their own resource needs, many providers or potential providers – regeneration agencies, local authorities, trusts and private sector companies – often do not have a very informed view of the resource needs of the community sector.

The aim of this section is to explore what a more systematic approach to resource provision could mean in practice.

A resource audit

For provision to be systematically organised, the first step would be to carry out a survey of existing resources in an area and their availability and accessibility in relation to the expressed needs of the community and voluntary sector. From this comparison, key gaps in provision could be identified and an action plan developed as part of a wider area-based capacity building strategy (this is discussed later). This whole process is called a resource audit. Obviously this could be carried out relating to the needs of just one specific group which would be a useful process.

However, a resource audit has more impact if carried out across a whole area or network of groups. The expressed needs for resources in capacity building could be established through a comprehensive survey of organisations and groups in the area. Information on how to do this is contained in several practical publications listed below.

'Our resource audit collected so much information that we were overwhelmed with the details. It wasn't categorised very clearly so it was hard to extract anything of use'.
Community liaison officer

Such a survey of needs and available resources could be carried out using personal visits, telephone research or postal questionnaire. In practice, collecting the information will usually involve a combination of all three; it is a question of deciding what balance you want and can afford in terms of time and money. Logically, it would be more effective to survey expressed needs for resources in the community sector first, and only then carry out a survey of available resources based on the results. In practice, it may not be possible to neatly separate the two. In designing a survey of available resources it is important to be clear as the aims of your audit and how you will collate and use the information once collected.

An audit of resource needs and availability can itself be a useful developmental tool to open up new resources. For example, in compiling the Calderdale Resource Guide, the questionnaire used for the survey specifically asked probing questions to resource holders, as to how their resources could be made more available to the community and voluntary sector. In response to this (and some gentle persuasion!) some community centres changed their policy on the availability of space and equipment.

The production of a resource guide could be one output arising from this audit, though this would obviously have to be integrated into the design of the audit from the start. The process of how to produce a resource guide has already been fully described elsewhere (Skinner 1995).

The compilation and publication of resource guides can contribute to the regeneration initiative in a number of ways:

- Increase the ability of groups to participate by increasing access to information
- Value local achievements and identities by celebrating the area as a multi-cultural community
- Build local networks by helping to put people in touch
- Increase locally-based economic development activity by encouraging use of local services and enterprises.

Activities and associated resource needs

Resource needs are more clearly understood if divided into categories, depending on the area of activity of community organisations. Here is a proposed set of categories; obviously, in practice there will be some overlap and blurring between them.

Communications
Access to or ownership of computers with word processing, spreadsheet, database and desktop publishing programs; laser printers; printing equipment; photocopier, fax and franking machines; presentation materials and display boards; overhead projectors, flip chart paper, video equipment, etc.

Management activities
Books and videos on management methods; information on financial planning, licensing and partnership structures; access to low-cost auditors; technical advice; secretarial assistance; access to funding information; access to low cost and supportive banking, etc.

Equal opportunities initiatives
Information on relevant legislation, recruitment and selection procedures; translators, signers; grant aid to make buildings accessible; portable hearing loops; access to Braille production; space, staff and equipment for crèches, for meetings and courses.

Project development
Advice on business planning; information on funding sources; legal information; professional advice from architects, landscape designers, planners, environmental specialists; information on how the council works; access to rooms and halls for consultation and public meetings, launches and celebrations.

General activities
Cheap stationery; office furniture; a modern telephone system; office space; meeting space; cheap insurance; publications on capacity building and community development; access to the Internet.

'Many community organisations were unable to obtain easy access to information concerning local authority grants and policies, government bills and circulars, training material, publications, journals and conference material.'

From a survey of community organisations in Scotland
(Purcell and Brown 1995).

What centres and institutions can do

The audit of resource needs and resource availability can lead to an action plan with recommendations on increased provision. Resources for capacity building can be provided in two main ways:

Centre-based provision

Here are some examples:

- Centres that can offer space and resources: community centres, community schools, arts centres, leisure centres, social clubs, religious centres, community enterprises and housing offices. Assistance could be provided in the form of a community resources room or area, or a policy of access to equipment.

  For example in north Hull, the Housing Action Trust has opened a resource centre in its own building offering computer facilities to local community organisations, with desktop publishing and Funder Finder programmes.

- Centres that can offer information and communication access: CABs, business advice centres, libraries and other information centres could broaden their information base to include capacity building information and increased access to information technology

- Purpose-built centres offering a fully comprehensive range: a new network of tailor-made resource centres could be established to complement existing provision; these centres could in turn have a servicing and 'satellite' support role for other centre-based resource provision described above.

In Barnsley, the borough council has established a number of resource centres to support self employment, vocational training and community-based capacity building. The Acorn Centre in Grimethorpe, for example, in addition to these roles, aims to involve community organisations in the management of facilities.

Institutional-based provision

In addition to this centre-based approach to resource provision there is the wider issue of agencies, organisations, private companies and institutions in the area developing a culture of access and interaction with the community and voluntary sector. Here are some examples:

- A local company makes its boardroom available to community organisations for high-profile presentation events

- A voluntary sector agency, in upgrading its photocopier, donates the (still useful) old one to a community organisation

- The local authority opens up its own resource of translators and signers for use by community groups

- An association of professional architectural firms offer free advice to community groups.

What the private sector can do

Here is a checklist of ways in which companies can support capacity building for community organisations by providing access to resources:

☐ Arrange access to company in-house services such as word processing, desktop publishing, photocopying or other services relevant to the company

☐ Offer access to meeting rooms and other similar facilities for training events, meetings, presentations, launches or 'away days'

☐ Give access to company in-house training courses that are already running

☐ Provide staff from the training section to offer short term specific forms of assistance such as training needs assessments

☐ Give support in kind, either new or surplus stock items or second-hand furniture and equipment

☐ Provide access to useful contacts and business forums.

For other options for the private sector, see Part 2 on mentoring, secondments and volunteering schemes.

The professional firms groups

A scheme has been established by Business in the Community where professional firms give a certain amount of free time and expertise to community and voluntary organisations in their area. The professional practices involved include surveyors, architects, accountants, solicitors, consulting engineers, public relations specialists and management and information technology consultants. The professional firms undertake assignments which include feasibility studies, structural surveys, marketing and business plans, legal and accountancy advice and property valuations. There is now a national network of 25 professional firms groups, comprising more than 400 members between them, providing well over £1 million worth of professional time to voluntary and community groups every year. Professional firms groups will work with any community-based, not-for-profit organisation working for social and economic regeneration of their local area, although there are certain qualifications.

For further information contact:
Business in the Community, telephone: 0171-224 1600.

Assisting community enterprises

An important further area of potential is between companies and community enterprises. For example The Body Shop International PLC has contributed to capacity building through its Community Trade Programme. It works closely with groups to enable them to build and sustain product development, quality control, planning, marketing and many other skills so that they can meet The Body Shop's buying standards, as well as stand alone in the market-place. While much of this work has been on an international basis, especially with communities in Third World countries, this innovative and useful model of capacity building could be extended to relationships between companies and community enterprises in Britain.

*For more information contact the Fair Trade Department,
The Body Shop International, telephone: 01903 731500.*

Approaching companies

Getting resources for capacity building will involve making approaches to companies. How can this be carried out most effectively? Companies receive many requests for financial support; requests that do not require hard cash, as listed above, are likely to receive a warmer response. When making a request it's worth approaching the company with a proposal rather than a begging letter, and consider what benefits there may be for the company such as staff development or publicity and obviously, an attractive, well thought out proposal will be looked upon more favourably.

'Capacity building has got to work both ways – the private sector needs to understand what community involvement really means.'
Black community leader

Experience has shown that a little research can produce more effective results. It's useful to find out if the company has a community involvement policy and if your organisation fits into the preferred areas of activity. If not, do not waste your time. It's also worth finding out the name of the contact person; there may be a community affairs manager but other staff members could be appropriate, depending on the type of request you are making. Invite these people to visit you and your organisation to see for themselves what you are doing – they could well return to their company enthused about your work.

Networking

Networking is a key way in which community organisations can share contacts, skills and information, and co-ordinate their activities. In this brief section, we examine practical ways in which community organisations can build such links and how regeneration agencies can support this.

Networking is especially important in capacity building because a fundamental feature is that it involves community groups themselves sharing knowledge and experience rather than relying on outside trainers, advisers or consultants. The question is – how does this process happen in practice and what needs to be done to enable its development?

The scope of networking

First, let's define the range of functions it can include (Gilchrist 1995). This is especially worth doing in networking as it is a term that suffers from overuse:

- Exchanging information and views
- Joint working on a campaign to mobilise support and influence policy
- Co-ordination of work in one area or district so as to avoid unnecessary duplication
- Exchanging skills and learning
- Giving support and confidence
- Developing a sense of common purpose
- Representing an area or interest group in a consultation or partnership.

Networks are important ways for minority groups to relate to each other without losing their own identity.

'When asked about training events and conferences that they had attended, community representatives often said that the best part of the event was the informal conversations' (Purcell and Brown 1995).

A useful definition of networking is:

'Networks – including associations, movements and coalitions – are semi-formal groupings in which each member organisation remains autonomous in its activities, but where enough common ground exists to establish shared agendas. Networks are rarely rigid or hierarchical and are an implicit challenge to territorial or possessive attitudes towards the handling of information and power. Dynamic networks may see diversity as their source of strength. At the same time they powerfully demonstrate that collaboration and co-operation are essential to development' (Eade and Williams 1995).

In practice networks can involve a variety of practical activities: the exact mix will depend on the aim of the network:

- mailings of information and newsletters
- regular meetings
- training workshops
- informal socials and celebrations
- electronic communication via e-mail and the Internet
- exchange visits and exchange placements
- conferences.

Assisting networks: what agencies and funders can do

Funders and regeneration agencies could consider offering assistance in the following range of ways:

- free use of meeting rooms
- servicing meetings
- providing a mailout service
- providing free or subsidised printing
- assisting with design of newsletters and leaflets
- community worker support.

There are a number of key points for regeneration agencies to consider when they are involved in assisting networks. For example, does the assistance itself dominate the networking process? Does the assistance come with strings attached? Do regeneration agency staff only encourage networks between groups they feel comfortable with? Will they be able to maintain their level of assistance if the network grows and changes its role?

For their part, community organisations need to be clear early on what they want from the link with other groups, what role the link will have, and what assistance, if any, they want to run the network. Members of each group involved in links through networks may need help to develop the skills and systems for reporting and being accountable to the base group.

Networks are important ways for minority groups to relate to each other without losing their own identity.

Case study
The Pan-London Capacity Building Programme

This case study is an example of a network taking a key role in the development of grassroots regeneration initiatives in London.

A Pan-London Community Regeneration Consortium has been established to develop a network of agencies which will provide capacity building for voluntary and community sector organisations involved in funding bids, including SRB and European sources, across London. Through this network the Pan-London Consortium will provide both tailor-made and course-based training as well as information, support and consultancy time. The overall aim is to strengthen the involvement of local communities in regeneration partnerships. The network itself is a pool of providers from the community and voluntary sector, TECs and the private sector. Each provider has specialist experience, knowledge and technical skills in training and organisational development or is contributing resources such as use of training suites.

The Consortium has received SRB Challenge Fund funding, from the Government Office for London. During the lifetime of the programme the Consortium aims to deliver 1,110 training weeks and give assistance to 502 voluntary organisations and 863 community groups, at least 30 per cent of which will be from the black and minority ethnic communities. Half of the organisations worked with will have ten staff or less, to ensure the emphasis is on organisations that need most support.

To achieve these objectives the programme will consist of a range of projects, including:

- Information and briefing for voluntary and community sector groups about partnerships and bidding processes
- Consultancy for groups wishing to be involved in developing partnerships
- Tailor-made training based on an ongoing assessment of training needs
- Technical bid support for groups involved in SRB programmes
- Management training for groups in existing regeneration schemes
- Financial and management training for key local individuals
- Support for the London Regeneration Network for voluntary and community sectors
- Specific development work with black and minority ethnic organisations
- Training for partnership boards, to build their capacity to develop links and work between different sectors.

The Consortium also has an exit strategy by planning in years five to seven of the programme a mentoring scheme, whereby groups already trained will be linked to groups who are selected for training in those years. It is also committed to identifying a specific number of development agencies and local partnerships across London to whom the work can be transferred at a more local level, both during and after the end of the programme.

For more information contact: Pan-London Community Regeneration Consortium, telephone 0171-820 3943.

Participative structures

Participation by community sector organisations in regeneration programmes can happen in a number of ways (DoE 1995):

- Involvement in the bidding process. This can be a contribution to deciding on strategic objectives, key elements and delivery structures for the bid

- Involvement in the design and management of projects, including identifying needs, planning and evaluation. Community involvement can vary depending on the stage reached in the project's development process

- Involvement in programme management, as well as programme monitoring and the development of a forward strategy. This will usually involve community representation at board level or involvement in implementation groups.

Capacity building needs to be more than a process of enhancing skills and developing structures; it is also about an ability to influence.

However for participation to be meaningful rather than token, it should commence prior to the bidding process. As demonstrated in many cases of bid preparation for rounds of the SRB Challenge Fund, the bidding process is too late a stage for involvement and an effective contribution. If local authorities, TECs and statutory agencies are serious about participation, there is a case for building participative structures and partnerships before this point has been reached.

The benefits of participation

Involvement by community organisations in bidding, programme and project management will obviously require considerable investment from the regeneration agency and statutory agencies active in the areas concerned, in terms of both resources and commitment. What are the possible advantages, then, of community involvement?

The Department of Environment suggests four main benefits:

- *Recognition of citizen's rights:* that communities have the right to negotiate their relationships with service providers and ultimately be involved in decision directly affecting them

- *Better decision making:* for example, that local people can contribute to the understanding of problems or needs in the area

- *More effective programme delivery:* for example, in that community organisations may be able to contribute resources not available to statutory bodies. This could be money raised from trusts or businesses, or be voluntary time and effort

- *Increased sustainability of the regeneration programme:* for example, through the development of locally-based delivery organisations that continue beyond the time limited nature of the programme. Sustainability was discussed in Part 1.

From the perspective of capacity building, there are in addition two other specific benefits arising from involvement in participative structures. These are:

'Our Small Projects Fund where residents join with professionals to decide on local grant applications has been a useful way for us all to learn new skills around funding and appraising projects.'
Canterbury Partnership Trust, Bradford

- The effective involvement of the community in the regeneration initiative is itself an aspect of capacity building. Increased influence is itself an integral part of a capacity building strategy. As argued in Part 2 in exploring definitions of empowerment, capacity building needs to be more than a process of enhancing skills and developing internal structures; it is also about an ability to influence, and for communities to have a direct impact on decisions directly affecting them (Fordham, 1995).

- Participative structures themselves can be a very effective environment within which skills, confidence, knowledge and understanding can be enhanced and expanded. Some regeneration agencies, such as Batley City Challenge, have consciously used participative forums as one way to create opportunities where community representatives can increase their organisational abilities.

Levels of participation

In establishing participative structures, regeneration agencies and participating organisations need to be clear as to the level of control that is being shared. A useful framework has been developed by Wilcox (1994) with five different levels, reflecting varying degrees of control within a ladder of participation:

- *Supporting independent community initiatives:* Assisting others to do what they want, perhaps within a framework of grant aid, advice and support provided by the resource holder

- *Acting together:* Not only do different interests decide what is best, but they form a partnership to carry it out

- *Deciding together:* Encouraging others to provide some additional ideas and options, and join in deciding on the best way forward

- *Consultation:* Offering a number of options and listening to the feedback

- *Information:* Informing people what has already been planned.

'Are professionals willing and able to give people in the community information to contribute to difficult decisions about the allocation of resources?'
Community liaison officer

The lower level of participation keeps the control with the agency but will probably result in less commitment from other parties. Only the top three levels involve substantial participation. Wilcox suggests different levels are appropriate for different circumstances; it's a case of horses for courses! What is important is that community organisations are not misled by resource holders into expecting a higher level of participation than is available in reality. This process – which has happened many, many times in communities – leads to alienation and loss of interest.

Guidelines for effective community participation in the context of urban regeneration have been usefully explored in several publications, as listed below in Further reading.

Different levels of participation are appropriate for different circumstances; it's a case of horses for courses!

A number of different models are now evolving of how community sector interests can be represented in the decision-making structures of regeneration agencies. One example is the Netherton SRB Partnership.

Case study
Netherton SRB Partnership

This case study describes an SRB Partnership with a high level of community representation and involvement.

In Netherton, Merseyside, the Partnership Board was established in May 1995 and has received over £8 million of SRB Challenge Funds. It is made up of :

- Three councillors, one from each main party
- Four business, one health authority and one TEC representative
- Five community sector representatives.

In addition to the Board, there is a Community Forum in the area involved in the regeneration initiative. Forum meetings are held regularly and are open to any community organisations in the area. Each community organisation gets one vote at the Forum meetings.

The Forum has five sub-groups dealing with the themes of crime, the environment, housing, education and training and community development. The chairperson of each sub-group is also the Board representative. Each sub-group is made up of volunteer members from the Community Forum, based on their own interests and skills. The sub-groups play a key part in consultation and feedback on local issues and priorities.

In particular, sub-group members are also involved in project steering groups which initiate and oversee the development of individual projects within the regeneration programme. Each project steering group is made up of three to four community representatives from the appropriate sub-group, including the chairperson. Other members of each project steering group are the appropriate programme manager, the managing agent and other interested parties.

The community representatives of project steering groups report back on a regular basis to the appropriate sub-group. Information on projects is then assimilated by a wider membership, allowing the community to gauge the appropriateness and effectiveness of each project. This process enables the community to co-ordinate projects and activities and leads to linkages and areas of integration.

This structure has enabled some meaningful involvement by the community. In addition, a particularly notable feature is that the Partnership Board membership has nominated one of the chairs of a sub-group to be the chair of the Board itself. Netherton is exceptional in this regard, in that the chair of the Partnership Board is a direct representative of the community sector.

For more information contact: the Netherton Partnership Board, telephone: 0151 330 5800.

Assessing progress on partnership working

Partnerships, either at district or local level, seem to have become widespread as structures to draw in and use a number of funding programmes,

including both the SRB Challenge Fund and many programmes within European Structural Funds. A new tool has been developed to assist in checking the performance of partnerships, called the Organisation Check for Partnerships. This is a pack containing a carefully designed questionnaire, divided into four sections covering: managing the service; managing finance; managing people and managing information. Each section has several sub-sections. For example, managing the service invites a examination of:

- purpose
- management committees
- working in a committee
- training needs
- administration and reception
- premises and equipment.

Each heading has boxes to indicate a satisfaction rating of one to four, as well as space for comments. A summary sheet at the end enables a score total and overall assessment of the organisation's performance. The questions for each heading will no doubt produce many a moan at Board level, reflecting many of the classic agonies of joint working:

- Has the main purpose has been clearly set out?
- Does everyone knows what they should be doing?
- Do we know in what direction we want to go over the next three years?
- Are there are clearly-defined and constructive relationships with other organisations?

While the check could be used on a DIY basis, using a facilitator produces more effective results. The tool is a checklist written to cater for a variety of partnerships and, as with any checklist, may need adapting to the needs of any one particular setting. The Organisation Check for Partnerships was developed in Barnsley, commissioned by Voluntary Action Barnsley and Northern College.

Copies can be obtained for £5 from: Val Harris Training,
telephone 01274 582191.

Participative structures:
What the regeneration agency can do

A more specific issue is the ways in which a regeneration agency can provide support for capacity building, in relation to community participation in the regeneration initiative.

Supporting meaningful participation

This could include:

- Transport and child care costs for participants to get to meetings

- A budget to pay for accessible meeting venues so a variety of community-based locations can be used, rather than just a large hall or the 'board room'

- Provision of information in an accessible form such as newsletters and directories

- Consultation events that may involve imaginative and innovative publicity events

- Provision for people with disabilities such as signers or large print versions of documents

- Provision to support black and ethnic minority participants such as translated publicity, halal meat available at lunches, etc.

- Generally addressing inequalities of power and status between the regeneration agency and community organisations.

Access to administrative support

This could include:

- Access to word processors, photocopiers and printers

- A typing and printing service for notes, minutes, reports, newsletters

- Access to a telephone, fax, e-mail and the Internet

- Practical help with organising community-based elections and opinion surveys.

Care needs to be taken in how such administrative resources are made available. Providing officer time for minute-taking at locally-based partnership meetings may be useful but of limited use if the minutes are not presented in accessible language and are dominated by the agency's own agenda.

Access to training specifically concerned with participation

This could include content that addresses:

- The nature of the regeneration agency's procedures, timetable and the obligations of government funding

- programme and project target setting, monitoring and evaluation

- the meaning of participation, including levels and structures

- practical skills involved in community representation, feedback and committee work

- the meaning of community development and area-based regeneration.

Despite an increasingly voiced interest in participation issues, both by community organisations and regeneration agencies, it is surprising how little such training is actually happening. Many forms of training needs analysis also focus on individual or organisational needs, and ignore or minimalise training needs associated with involvement in participative structures.

Involvement by community organisations as consultees, decision makers and joint actors in local projects, partnerships and regeneration programmes often requires a sophisticated level of skill, knowledge and ability. They are being asked to contribute to the management or development of schemes and services that have challenged far more better-resourced and better-informed agencies! Meaningful involvement will take time, use resources and yes, challenge existing practices. It also requires ongoing support at neighbourhood and network level. We now move on consider this process.

Community development support

Community development support can take a variety of forms carried out by a range of statutory and voluntary sector agencies in any one area, as well as by the regeneration agency itself. This variety of forms is returned to later; in this section our main area of focus is on the most tangible form of support – the direct employment of community workers. Community work involves a range of methods and skills, solidly based in a strong and explicit value base. A current definition of community work is given below. In addition to their wider aims and activities, the particular area of interest here is – what roles do community workers have in the context of capacity building and community infrastructure? These roles can be defined as:

• To give groups ongoing support

• To assist in building participative structures

• To ensure equality of involvement

• To enable the setting up of new groups

• To develop voluntary community work involvement

• To provide specialist skills.

These are now explored in turn.

Give groups ongoing support

As discussed in Part 2, capacity building, as well as involving the development of skills, concerns personal development, individual change and increased confidence. To be effective this process need not only be associated with specific inputs of training programmes or usually time-limited assistance involved in organisational development. In other words, community workers – whose skill especially lie in the area of personal empowerment – have an essential role to play in providing an on going support process.

Assist in building participative structures

Underlying the review of participative structures in the last section is the importance of the ability of community organisations to influence and communities to have a direct impact on decisions directly affecting them. The building of participative structures and the skills of organisations involved in them – both community groups and agencies – takes time and is itself a developmental process. In particular, as argued in the last section, meaningful participation in regeneration initiatives requires preparatory work in potential target areas prior to the bidding process. For example, on the Canterbury estate in Bradford, three years of community work support helped to build the strength of a key residents' association that then bid and obtained a substantial sum from the Bradford Task Force, to form the Canterbury Partnership Trust. Now that the trust is established and a specific two-year training programme is in place, community work support is still needed to build and maintain estate-based involvement in the board and its sub-committees with a real sense of ownership and confidence.

Ensure equality of involvement in capacity building programmes

Equality has been a continuing underlying theme in this publication. For a number of reasons, some community groups may have had little contact with the regeneration programme in their area or associated capacity building activities and may feel marginalised and alienated by this process. Outreach work may be needed to build relationships with such groups, to ensure their views are being heard on how provision could be adapted to their needs. Such relationship-building work requires cultural sensitivity and the growth of trust, and cannot always be tied to the agenda of training programmes or organisational change.

Enable the setting up of new groups

The establishment of new community groups, perhaps prioritising parts of the neighbourhood or community in general where collective involvement is low, is a key aspect of the regeneration process. Capacity building can be a useful element in this demanding activity which often involves direct work with individuals and local networks. Capacity building in such settings may itself be flexibly and informally arranged, involving small groups in the early stages of organising and teamwork. This type of grassroots neighbourhood work is essential to avoid the pitfall of regeneration agencies responding mainly to already well-established and more articulate groups.

Develop voluntary community work involvement

Many paid community workers adopt an important role of supporting the skill development of unpaid community workers – locally-based organisers and campaigners who have a valuable resource of skills and experience to offer their own areas. This resource can itself make a significant contribution to community life and is in need of support to both recognise and develop it. Community workers, apart from acting as role models in some respects, can help to steer people towards learning programmes and accredited courses in community work, as described in Part 2.

Offer specialist skills in capacity building

An increasing number of practising community workers over the last decade have developed training skills as a part of their skill base, as reflected in the growth of the Federation of Community Work Training Groups. Also, as discussed in Part 3, community workers can be specialists in certain areas of organisational development such as team work, grounding, resource audits and so on. Apart from the value of these skills

Effective community work at neighbourhood and network level can be seen as the essential building blocks to any capacity building programmes.

in their own right, a key issue here is that they can be used within the context of existing relationships with community organisations in any one neighbourhood or network. These relationships can provide access and opportunities for capacity building, which some less-confident groups will experience in no way other than delivered by their known and trusted local community worker!

'As we see it, the community work service forms the building blocks for effective capacity building programmes.' Community work manager

Overall there is a strong case for properly-resourced community work provision to complement the main capacity building initiative; effective community work at neighbourhood and network level can be seen as the essential building blocks to any capacity building programmes. Specific programmes addressing skills, structures and systems in the community sector need to be established in addition to – and not as a substitute for – an ongoing and well-organised community work input.

Community work

The following draft Definition of Community Work, developed by the England Interim Board for Community Work Training and Qualifications, describes the aims and objectives towards which both paid and unpaid community workers work.

Community Work aims to:
Promote co-operation and encourage the process of participatory democracy by:

- Supporting new and existing community groups to work on issues of common interest and concern
- Seeking to create links and liaisons between groups and individuals within a locality, around issues of common concern on a basis of mutual respect, whilst recognising diversity and differences
- Promoting the development of alliances and the recognition of collective action by encouraging people to reflect and act together in order to achieve common goals, and influence decision makers
- Acknowledging the specific experience and contribution of all individuals in communities, to enable people to enhance their capacity to play a role in shaping and determining the society of which they are part
- Promoting models of partnership and organisational structures which empower communities.

Encourage self-determination by:

- Helping individuals and community groups to define their own objectives
- Supporting individuals and groups to run their autonomous and collectively-managed projects
- Develop appropriate organisational forms to ensure self-determination.

Ensure the sharing and development of knowledge by:

- Developing awareness and understanding of issues and perspectives through social, economic and political change
- Enabling people to develop the expertise and skills necessary to further their own objectives
- Enabling people to recognise the values within which they work.

Change the balance of power and power structures in ways which will facilitate local democracy, challenge inequalities and promote social justice by:

- Recognising that the unequal distribution of power is both a personal and political issues, and that Community Work has a responsibility for linking the personal learning which empowers people, through to the collective learning and action for change which empowers communities

- Recognising oppression within society and the necessity to confront all forms of oppression, both within ourselves and within society

- Taking the lead in confronting the attitudes and behaviour of individuals, groups and institutions which discriminate against and disempower people, whether as individuals or groups

- Pursuing the above through the adoption and promotion of explicit anti-discriminatory policies and practices.

Community development support: what agencies and local authorities can do

Many local authorities are now developing corporate community development policies affecting the style and nature of service delivery. Both practice and policy issues have been discussed in a useful AMA publication (AMA 1993). Here we offer a checklist of options for regeneration agencies, local authorities, statutory agencies and voluntary sector organisations in terms of community development support:

- Ensure provision of community work input into target areas prior to bid preparation

- Ensure there is adequate information on how community groups can contact and use community workers both those based in the regeneration agency itself and in other agencies in the area

- Maintain appropriate community work staffing levels throughout the duration of the regeneration programme

- Ensure liaison between community workers and staff and agencies involved in providing capacity building programmes

- Support networks and training programmes both for paid and unpaid community workers

- Integrate community work into the continuation strategy to support post-programme structures and systems

- Ensure front-line staff involved in service delivery and direct contact with groups receive support, management and training to enhance their ability to relate to the community sector.

This last point leads on to the also important issue of the openness of professional staff to engage in the process. We now move on to explore this issue.

Professional capacity building

'Funders need to learn and build their capacities and shift to meet the needs of groups; the learning and adjustments should not all be one way.'
The Oxford Conference

As well as changing structures, capacity building also involves developing new attitudes, skills and processes in the regeneration agencies themselves. This activity is called professional capacity building. As well as the regeneration agency, it obviously applies equally well to managers and staff at all levels in other service delivery organisations such as the local authority, the health authority, housing associations, professional voluntary sector organisations and other statutory agencies.

The experience of many community groups, in interacting with statutory organisations and agencies, is often one of frustration at bureaucratic responses and a lack of understanding. At officer level community groups may be seen as a time-consuming hindrance, uninformed amateurs who have no place in the professional planning process. At elected member level in local authorities, community organisations may be viewed as a threat to members' own power base.

'Real change needs both sides of the coin.'
Community worker

Professional capacity building is the other side of the coin to community-based capacity building. Unless capacity building strategies involve both aspects, community organisations will, in effect, be blocked and limited in their ability to contribute to the regeneration initiative.

Professional capacity building: what agencies and local authorities can do

Practices by managers and staff in statutory agencies and organisations that can enhance community involvement and participation include:

- *Sharing information*: officers can adopt an openness to systematically share information on, for example, the structure of their organisation, funding timetables and criteria, and corporate procedures and priorities. Some agencies have produced handbooks on how their organisation works available to the voluntary and community sector

- *Sharing contacts:* names and addresses of useful contacts; information on contact people for access to resources, facilities, equipment. Again, some agencies have produced contact/resource directories

- *Sharing skills*: officers often have a variety of skills that can as appropriate be shared with members of community organisations. This may be, for example, through jointly preparing a grant application or appraisal report on a project

'When mainstream agencies talk to residents, residents are expected to do all the changing. Agencies need to turn themselves inside out.'
Researcher

- *Recognising community organisations have a role to play:* this is perhaps more fundamental than specific activities described so far. Staff need to accept that the community sector has a valid, integral and lasting contribution to make to the regeneration process. This attitudinal change is enhanced if led by the chief executive and chairperson in the regeneration agency.

In order to enable the process of professional capacity building what forms of support and training could be developed? Broadly, as in community-based capacity building, the activities will fall into the two main areas of developing people and developing organisations.

Developing people

The content of training could include:

- Understanding community development – levels of participation, the nature of the community sector and the values involved in community work

- Developing communication skills – listening skills, the ability to converse with people from a wide variety of backgrounds, the ability to explain technical terms in a user-friendly manner and avoiding jargon when unnecessary

- Developing meeting and decision making skills – understanding and using decision making systems in a variety of settings, understanding the meaning of partnership working.

As in community-based capacity building, this learning process could take a variety of forms;

- An inter-departmental or inter-agency officer study group

- 'Away days' and tailor-made training for all board members

- Course-based training provision in-house, or in a local educational institution

- Mentoring from an experienced community activist

- Placements and visits to community organisations to see how they are organised and run

- Individual staff supervision specifically on professional capacity building.

Developing organisations

This could include:

- The formation of networks of managers and fieldwork staff to ensure an exchange of information and the development of roles and skills that encourage participation

- The encouragement for senior officers, managers and policy makers to participate in post-experience training programmes in community practice. A scheme to establish such a programme is being explored by CDF (Butcher and Henderson 1993).

- The development of a staff training plan that specifically addresses professional capacity building and is adopted by the board and actively promoted by the chief executive

- An organisational review of processes and procedures to assess to what extent these form unnecessary blocks to appropriate participation. This review could usefully involve a degree of user feedback.

'The third key task then is to undertake a skills training audit of those staff who have prime responsibility for working with the public. This will include both outreach and centre based staff and those responsible for community liaison in their various departments' (AMA 1993).

Further reading

Association of Metropolitain Authorities (1993) *Local Authorities and Community Development: A strategic opportunity for the 1990s*, AMA.

Butcher, H. and Henderson, P. (1993) *Training for Community Practice*, Report of a consultation. Copies available from CDF North, telephone 0113 2460909.

DoE (1995) *Involving the Community in Urban and Rural Regeneration*, HMSO.

Eade, D, and Williams, S. (1995) *The Oxfam Handbook of Development and Relief*, vol. I, Oxfam.

Flecknoe, C. and McLellan, N. (1994) *The What, Why and How of Neighbourhood Community Development*, Community Matters.

Gilchrist, A. (1995) Adapted from *Community Development and Networking*, CDF.

Hawtin, M. Huhes, G. and Percy-Smith, J. (1994) *Community Profiling: Auditing social needs*, Open University Press.

Purcell, R. and Brown, S. (1995) *New Directions: A summary of an enquiry into community organisations in Scotland*, Scottish Community Development Centre.

Skelcher, C. McCabe, A. Lowndes, V. Nanton, P. (1996) *Community Networks in Urban Regeneration: 'It all depends on who you know'*, The Policy Press.

Wilcox, D. (1994) *The Guide to Effective Participation*, Partnership.

Part 5
Developing Plans and Strategies

The aims of Part 5 are to:

• Describe options on how to devise and prepare a capacity building strategy at area level

• Describe how to devise and prepare a capacity building plan with a community organisation

• Explore approaches to the evaluation of capacity building activities.

As can be seen, plans refer to capacity building at group or project level whereas strategies refer to capacity building at area level. Obviously an informed area-based strategy would consider and be partly based on locally-based capacity building plans. First we examine how capacity building strategies can be devised and implemented, and recommend a five roles framework for prioritising the allocation of resources.

Developing an area-based strategy

'An area-based strategy would need to be devised through a widespread process of community consultation.'
Community work manager

In this context, a strategy is a set of priorities and objectives for the development of capacity building over the long term, based on the regeneration needs of an area. While such an overview may be initiated by a regeneration agency, to be effective its production will need to include consultation with and the involvement of a broad range of community and voluntary organisations.

Ideally, the process of devising an area-based capacity building strategy would involve the following steps to gather information:

• *Needs:* an examination of the nature of the community and voluntary sectors in the area and in particular their training, organisational development needs and community infrastructure needs

• *Plans:* consideration of any existing capacity building plans devised by voluntary and community organisations

• *Provision:* a review of existing capacity building provision and activities

• *Regeneration strategy:* an examination of the overall regeneration strategy for the area in the light of the above elements.

An area-based capacity building strategy would consequently be developed out of and operate in parallel to the broader regeneration strategy but, as stated, in the light of existing needs, plans and existing provision. Following this process of information gathering and review, decisions will need to be made regarding how and where resources for capacity building are directed. We now suggest a way of approaching this.

The five roles framework

We believe that an area-based capacity building strategy can be developed effectively by using the five roles framework. The five roles framework is an adaptation and development of a model of five roles for the community described in CDF's publication 'Regeneration and the Community' (CDF 1996). This strategic framework proposes:

- That the community has five main roles to play in regeneration
- Each of these roles will have particular capacity building needs associated with them as well as overlapping and shared needs
- That both community organisations and regeneration agencies can use an awareness of these roles to decide on priorities in capacity building provision.

'The five roles offer a useful framework to understand what is happening in an area in terms of group-based activity.'
Community work manager

The five roles for the community in regeneration are:
- Beneficiaries and users of services
- Consultees and representatives of local opinion
- A focus of general community activity
- Deliverers of services and generators of community economic development
- Potential long-term partners in regeneration.

We now explore each of these five roles for the community in more detail, and in each case examine the possible implications for capacity building provision for community organisations.

Role 1: the community as beneficiary and user

Regeneration schemes should benefit local people as individuals, for example as users of a community transport service, and as participants in vocational training. Equally, community organisations themselves can be beneficiaries and users, for example a community association runs a youth project in a new community hall provided by a regeneration programme. For regeneration schemes to succeed, a basic minimum requirement is simply that local communities and locally-based organisations should benefit. That benefit is likely to be more substantial if regeneration schemes reflect real local needs. In this sense, community organisations can be supported to be active rather than passive consumers, feeding in a constructive and systematic manner their views on their own needs. They can also be informed users and beneficiaries, using information on resources and opportunities to make more effective choices.

For community organisations to be active and informed users and beneficiaries – that is to be active in Role 1 – capacity building support could include:

- Providing up-to-date information on local services, facilities and opportunities through, for example, the availability of directories and resource guides
- Arranging outreach work and group-based training to increase levels of participation in training

• To give support to community organisations in overcoming barriers to access as users of community buildings and facilities.

In Bethnal Green, for example, the City Challenge is engaged in initiatives to overcome physical barriers which prevent access to facilities and training provision for community organisations through schemes such as transport, child care and training grants. It is also involved in pro-active work to break down barriers between local people and educational institutions.

Role 2: the community as consultee and representative of local opinion

Partnerships and regeneration agencies need to consult the community to ensure regeneration programmes address real needs. Community organisations have a crucial role to play in representing local opinion on the needs of an area in relation to the planning and implementation of the regeneration programme. They can serve as a useful source of information, both on their own members' needs (as in Role 1 described earlier) and also on the wider needs of the area. In some cases, community organisations have formed networks or coalitions with well-established systems to represent the views of an area or particular interest groups.

In terms of capacity building as consultees and representatives, community sector organisations may want help to:

• Be more informed about participation levels and methods (Wilcox 1992)

• Increase their ability to clearly and democratically represent their own interests, neighbourhood or network

• Increase their presentation and organisational skills

• Generally become more skilled in understanding area-based regeneration and associated concepts and ideas

• Participate in consultations on local economic development

• Maintain their independent stance and campaigning work as appropriate.

Role 3: the community as a source of general community activity

Even without any specific relationship with the regeneration initiative, independent community activity is important in its own right.

The term 'general community activity' means locally-based informal voluntary involvement, for example in sports clubs, social clubs, parent and toddler groups, religious groups, neighbourhood carnivals, health education groups and so on. Much of this grassroots activity is informally run and may not at first sight appear to be relevant to regeneration programmes, especially compared with output-focused projects involving community enterprise, vocational training or job creation. However these networks, groups, clubs and activities provide the basic social environment from which more targeted initiatives can be built; they all help to provide personal support, confidence, contacts and skill development. They can be especially important during times of transition and change, for example in former coalfield areas.

Community organisations are also a part of this general community activity, though at one end of the spectrum, being generally larger and more structured than the average informal group active at this level.

Capacity building intending to strengthen this general community activity could, for example:

- Provide training to group leaders in facilitation skills
- Offer group-based tailor-made training sensitive to the needs of the particular setting
- Resource the formation of locally-based networks
- Resource larger community organisations as bases in their neighbourhood to act as 'satellite' support centres.
- Resource umbrella and servicing bodies that can offer support, information, representation and, in turn, their own capacity building provision, to smaller, less structured groups.

Role 4: the community as deliverer of services and generator of community economic development

Some community organisations seek to play a direct role in the delivery of services which may or may not be part of the regeneration programme. This role can take a variety of forms and operate at a variety of levels. They may alternatively or additionally help to stimulate community economic development. Here are some examples:

- A furniture recycling scheme which provides cheap reconditioned furniture for families on benefit
- A community café that develops a catering service for city-wide voluntary sector events
- A community-controlled vocational training centre
- An estate management board that manages local authority housing stock.

Initially those organisations in the voluntary and community sector most prepared to actually deliver services as part of the regeneration programme are likely to be professional voluntary organisations, such as charities specialising in a particular service. Because community sector organisations are often totally 'voluntary' in nature, without (or with only part-time) paid staff, they may need additional capacity building assistance to participate in service delivery. Local residents, as volunteers, may often manage projects in their spare time and, in adopting a delivery role, community organisations may be taking on new, demanding responsibilities. There are advantages to community organisations becoming directly involved in service provision. They often have an inside knowledge of at least some part of the local community and also can build up community strengths and volunteering capacity; there is, consequently, a dual value in allocating parts of the programme to them.

Some community organisations quite rightly do not want to become involved in service delivery or community enterprise. However, where they do wish to take on this role, community organisations could be assisted in capacity building in a number of ways, for example:

- A management development training programme (see the Hackney Community Training Programme as an example, p.55)

- Training and mentoring schemes in business planning and organisational skills (see the Hackney Community Mentoring Scheme, p.29)

- A grants scheme to enable groups to obtain specialist assistance with organisational development

- A support network and training programme on money management for boards of community enterprises

- Facilitation work with community enterprises that have lost touch with their local neighbourhood and need help with a process called 'grounding' to rebuild their local community base.

Role 5: community organisations as long-term partners

As argued in Part 1, the long-term sustainability of regeneration schemes requires the active involvement and ongoing commitment of the community and, in particular, locally-based community organisations. This can include participation in locally-based or area-based partnerships, as well as the building up of assets such as premises, equipment or endowment funds. Asset development can help to ensure activities continue at low cost or generate income to support existing new initiatives.

Here are some examples of locally-based partnerships and asset development initiatives:

- A neighbourhood-based development trust, managed primarily by local residents but involving local authority representation (see the Canterbury Partnership Trust on p.34 as an example)

- A community-controlled vocational training centre that acts as an external institution linked to a further education college (see Manor Training and Resource Centre on p.45 as an example)

- A community-based trust run by a coalition of residents' groups building up an endowment fund to sponsor local community enterprise.

Some of the implications of partnerships in terms of capacity building were discussed in Part 1. Particular forms of support for community organisations involved in partnerships and in locally-based asset management could be:

- Training and support in partnership working

- Information on models of partnerships, trusts and asset development

- Training and advice on financial management

- Information on and training in area-based regeneration strategies at policy and practice levels.

Using the five roles framework

The five roles provide a useful framework for the prioritising of capacity building provision on at least four levels. It can be used by:

- *A community organisation* in reviewing the set of roles in which it is active may decide to become involved in a new role. For example, a community association whose members are beneficiaries and whose management committee are already consultees in the regeneration programme now wishes to become a service deliverer. It negotiates funding for capacity building on this basis (see the Canterbury Partnership Trust case study on p.15 as an example of this). What is equally important is that any one community organisation may not want to become involved in any new role or be involved specifically with the regeneration initiative. It may require and ask for and obtain capacity building assistance to pursue its own ongoing aims and activities, and this is obviously a perfectly valid choice

- *A network of community and voluntary organisations* active in the regeneration area or further afield wishes to support its members in becoming more involved in service delivery and partnership roles. They negotiate funding to themselves to operate a capacity building programme on this basis (see the Pan-London Capacity Building Programme, p.92)

- *A regeneration agency* in terms of its own programme agenda and continuation strategy, identifies the need to increase the number of community organisations involved in specific roles. It consequently, after consultation, prioritises resources for capacity building to strengthen the development of these roles (see the Hackney Task Force case study, p.121)

- *a major funding programme* identifies the need to encourage bidders to strengthen community organisations in their area and their levels of activity in certain roles. It consequently uses the five roles framework to develop additional selection criteria (see the European Structural Funds case study, p.122).

While the five roles framework has this potential for use at any of these four levels, our main concern in this section is at regeneration agency level. We now look at the process of prioritising in more detail.

Priorities within the Strategy

'We are interested in using the five roles framework as a basis for appraising the level of development of community groups.'
A City Challenge manager

Bearing in mind the five potential roles, priority setting will consequently need to consider:

- Improving the effectiveness of community organisations within their existing sets of roles
- Enabling community organisations, when they decide they want to, to move between roles and in particular, adopt the more demanding roles of service delivery and partnership.

Priorities within the strategy need also to reflect two important principles. The principle of *equality,* ensuring for example:

- That capacity building reaches and supports newer, or less articulate groups rather than just the well-established and well-known voluntary and community organisations
- That the needs of groups who especially experience discrimination and deprivation are fairly represented.

The principle of *empowerment,* ensuring for example:

- That the whole process of devising a capacity building strategy has itself been participatory and consultative
- That empowerment as a way of working influences relationships between statutory agencies and organisations in the community.

Priorities will usually also have to reflect operational needs such as:

- The political needs for the regeneration agency to be seen to be providing a balance of resources between different neighbourhoods
- The operational needs of the regeneration programme itself, in terms of developing potentially under-resourced sectors of the community, e.g. arts, youth, elderly
- The operational needs of short term impact versus long term investment.

The five roles should not necessarily be seen as a hierarchy.

Consequently, we suggest that priorities in a capacity building strategy can be established through a balanced and informed consideration of roles and principles in the context of operational needs.

Discussion

As with any framework or model, the five roles framework needs to be used with care and adapted to both local needs and the particular aims of the regeneration programme. Within the regeneration area, the regeneration agency may hope to allocate resources in a developmental pattern over time, to reflect the growing strength of the voluntary and community sector to participate in, manage and deliver aspects of the regeneration programme. The five roles framework caters for this development, indicating the possibility of a different combination of forms of assistance for capacity building at different stages of the programme's life span.

'We want to be a strong community in our own right, which might mean in the end we don't join the partnership but go in a different direction. It seems to me that this is what community development is about.'
Community organiser

However it is important that the five roles should not necessarily be seen as a hierarchy which implies more resources should be directed to those active in the fourth or fifth role. Some community organisations may carry out very important functions in their neighbourhood without being directly involved in service delivery or partnership working. In addition, partnership working is certainly not the only form of involvement in the regeneration initiative; some groups may be very active and contribute substantially to their area but simply choose not to work closely with other agencies. This independence should be respected.

The development of an area-based strategy for capacity building is an essential element of any regeneration programme, especially given the importance of the need for sustainability so that the initiative creates lasting impact. Area-based strategies can also be linked to a unified, longer-term city-wide regeneration strategy. In this manner, capacity building as a theme has the potential to act as a common thread to link different rounds of bidding, for example in SRB Challenge Fund bids.

An important issue here is timing - when can or should the process of devising an area based capacity building strategy be carried out? To do this properly, involving both community sector consultation and a systematic assessment of training and organisational development needs, obviously requires a substantial input of time and resources. Only once such an assessment and consultation process is carried out can an effective area based strategy for capacity building be established. There are at least two main points when this process can occur:

- *During the initial phase of the regeneration programme period.* For example, as part of the Sandwell Regeneration Partnership's Round Two SRB Challenge Fund seven-year programme, a thorough assessment of the condition and development needs of the community sector has been carried out in the first year (CDF 1996). The main purpose of this study was to establish the baseline level and future resourcing needs for increased community involvement.

- *Prior to and during bid preparation.* There is a constraint here associated in the SRB Challenge Fund with the limited time period between identification of the proposed regeneration area, and the bid submission deadline. Even when the target area is known further in advance – as in some of the European Structural funds programmes – there is then the issue of the resource implications of such development work. In some cases this can be catered for by a far-sighted local authority that commits staff time and resources to address this need well in advance of the bid preparation stage.

More fundamentally this dilemma suggests the structure of the funding programmes themselves may need to be revised. For example, an examination of the effectiveness of the community economic development priority of the Objective Two funding programme (European Commission 1996) highlighted the need for a new 'Level One' priority. This would be a pre-conditions stage chiefly to build local capacity around pilot projects and facilitate involvement of people in the production of a local economic strategy. It is proposed a new Level Two priority would fund core projects, building on the local capacity and strategy developed through the Level One preparation. While this framework is specific to community economic development, it suggests a useful model that could be applied to other funding programmes, ensuring resources are available at the pre-bid preparatory phase to facilitate the involvement of the community sector in the generation of an effective area based capacity building strategy.

'Ideally the community and voluntary sector will take the lead in devising an area-based capacity building strategy.'
Community work manager

The development of an area-based strategy will obviously require an effective planning process, consulting all the major players involved in the regeneration initiative. We provide a checklist that can be photocopied and used at planning meetings with board members, regeneration agency staff and representatives of the voluntary and community sector etc. It is based on the contents of Parts Two, Three and Four as well as the Five Roles Framework. As with any checklist, it may need adapting to the particular setting and situation; and particular terms used in some of the questions may need explanation. Use of the checklist will usually identify a large number of areas where more information is needed before a coherent strategy can be devised. Consequently the process may need to be spread over several planning sessions with information gathering, research, consultation etc. carried out in a structured way between sessions.

Developing an area-based strategy for capacity building

This checklist can be used to assist community representatives, practitioners, regeneration agency staff and Partnership Board members in the work of preparing a strategy for capacity building in the regeneration area. When using this checklist the terms may need some introduction.

Assessing needs

☐ How have the *training* needs of the community and voluntary sectors been identified?

☐ How have the *organisational development* needs of the community and voluntary sectors been identified?

☐ What are the main findings arising from these assessments of *training and organisational development* needs?

☐ How has the existing level of *capacity building provision* been clarified?

☐ What *access to resources* do the community and voluntary sectors need for capacity building?

☐ Have *networking* needs for the community and voluntary sector been identified?

☐ Has the existing nature of *community development support* been assessed?

☐ Have needs for future *community development support* been clarified?

Establishing principles and priorities

☐ What are the overall *aims* of the capacity building programme?

☐ What *delivery mechanisms* for the capacity building programme will be used and why?

☐ What *roles* for the community in the regeneration initiative are being prioritised for capacity building support and why?

☐ How do these *priorities* relate to the aims and objectives of the main regeneration programme strategy itself?

☐ How is *equality* as an underlying principle being integrated into the capacity building provision?

☐ How is *empowerment* as an underlying principle being integrated into the capacity building provision?

Community consultation and involvement

☐ How are the voluntary and community sectors involved in devising the *aims and forms of delivery* of the capacity building strategy?

☐ Is the overall strategy for capacity building based on *capacity building plans* originating from grassroots community organisations?

Organising provision

☐ What *forms of training* will be selected and why?

☐ What sources of *assistance for organisational development* will be made more available and why?

☐ What *funding sources* – such as community chests – are being established to cater for rapid response to requests for assistance with capacity building preparation work?

☐ What *participative structures* are being established as learning environments and in what way is this learning being supported?

☐ How are *networks* relevant to capacity building being supported?

☐ How is *information on existing provision* and available forms of assistance for capacity building being distributed to the voluntary and community sector?

Professional capacity building

☐ What *needs analysis* has been carried out?

☐ What *training programmes* have been established in relation to identified needs?

☐ What process of *organisational change* is being pursued in relation to identified needs?

Evaluation

☐ How is *training provision* being monitored and evaluated?

☐ How is the use of *organisational development* assistance being monitored and evaluated?

☐ In what way will the *outcomes and targets* for the capacity building programme reflect the principles that underlie it?

☐ Will the evaluation involve both *hard and soft* information?

☐ How will the results of the evaluation be fed into the planning cycle for the capacity building programmes so as to allow changes in practice?

Implementing a capacity building strategy

We now explore in more detail how a capacity building strategy can be implemented. The key co-ordinator and resource provider for this task will usually be a regeneration agency, though it may alternatively be a network, when they have access to substantial resources. In this section we also give an example of capacity building strategies developed in relation to European Structural Funds.

Financial resources can be directed using a variety of delivery mechanisms, although in practice there are at least five main ways the regeneration agency can approach this, by:

- Developing special funding arrangements that encourage or request capacity building activities

- Directly operating capacity building programmes including employing specialist staff

- Commissioning capacity building programmes that are run by community and voluntary organisations or specialist agencies

- Establishing participative structures that stimulate the development of particular capacities

- Fast tracking – selecting a limited number of community organisations for prioritised support.

These five delivery mechanisms can be used to direct the agency's resources based on the priorities established within the capacity building strategy.

Developing special funding arrangements

The allocation of funding is obviously a powerful tool in any capacity building strategy. Here are some examples:

- A fund is established specifically to give voluntary and community organisations grants to finance capacity building. For example, the London Borough of Brent has created a fund where groups can apply for up to £5,000 to finance training and consultancy

- A grant aid scheme that offers revenue funding for the voluntary and community sector is established with the criteria that all applications have to demonstrate an element of capacity building in their proposed activities. For example, in Batley the City Challenge's Community Development Fund requests all applicants for community centre grants participate in a premises management training course.

- A capacity building funding budget is established with a scoring system in the selection criteria that favours applicants involved in particular roles. For example in Yorkshire and Humberside, the European Secretariat developed the Five Roles Framework to devise additional selection criteria for Priority Six, Objective Two bids (see the case study on Capacity Building and the European Structural Funds pp.122-123).

Capacity building development worker posts: guidelines on job descriptions

This is a checklist of possible areas of work that staff specifically involved in capacity building with the community and voluntary sector could be active in:

- Assist groups in identifying training needs

- Assist groups in identifying and assessing organisational development needs

- Help groups to devise their own plans for capacity building

- Organise training and locally-based learning programmes based on needs e.g. courses, visits, mentoring schemes, action-based learning schemes

- Assist groups in making good use of outside specialists and consultants

- Collect and disseminate information on the availability of training and specialist help

- Offer advice on appropriate structures of organisation e.g. community association, registered charity, development trust, limited company

- Help groups to develop business/action plans

- Assist groups in securing additional funding and resources e.g. equipment, office space, access to cheap printing

- Collect and disseminate information on funding and resources

- Enable groups to effectively take part in networks so as to exchange experience and build useful new links

- Help groups to understand and contribute to local economic development strategies

- Help groups to take part effectively in participative structures so as to contribute to decision making.

Principles that underlie these approaches are:

- Work in a way that builds confidence, shares information, develops skills and encourages initiative

- Consider and apply equal opportunities principles at all stages of organisation and activity.

Directly operating capacity building programmes

This can take a variety of forms:

- The regeneration agency directly employs staff who will carry out training, organisational development and community infrastructure development. See above for a checklist of options for a job description, for staff employed specifically with a capacity building role

- The regeneration agency directly sets up and runs a capacity building scheme. For example, in Bethnal Green, the City Challenge company itself has set up a pool of fundraising consultants and placed them with targeted community organisations involved in managing community arts centres.

Commissioning capacity building programmes

This is perhaps the most common form of delivery of capacity building. Here the regeneration agency contracts community or voluntary organisations or more specialist agencies to provide forms of training or organisational development.

- For example in Bradford, the Royds Community Association, an SRB Partnership has directly sponsored the provision of community work Stage 1 and Stage 2 training courses, to be run the West Yorkshire Community Work Training Group.

Establishing participative structures

Here the regeneration agency creates structures and establishes relationships that, in addition to carrying out a main organisational function, also create learning environments:

- The regeneration agency encourages and facilitates the formation of working groups and consultative committees specifically to develop skills in partnership working. For example, in Bradford on the Canterbury estate, a small projects committee involving local residents has been an opportunity to develop skills in project assessment and grant administration

- The regeneration agency negotiates small-scale service level agreements with community organisations who are new to the contract culture. In this way, the agency can directly develop more organisations to engage in a service delivery role, using this initial agreement as a springboard for them to take on more substantial contracts at a later date. For example, the London Borough of Brent is operating such a scheme with five community organisations in 1996/97, specifically as one aspect of its capacity building programme.

Fast tracking

Fast Tracking is a process where the regeneration agency in effect selects a specific number of community organisations and makes available additional resources for capacity building. Fast tracking in capacity building is usually adopted when there is a pressure on the regeneration agency to increase the pace of development and change, especially in relation to the implementation of a continuation strategy. The key issue in the adoption of a fast tracking process – and often a very controversial one – is the criteria on which the choice of groups is made. In practice, the same set of factors can be considered as in the process of setting priorities within the overall capacity building strategy, as discussed earlier:

- The enhancement of certain roles

- The principle of equality

- Operational needs.

For example in Batley, the City Challenge developed a fast tracking scheme that specifically included organisations which were:

- Representative of those sections of the community most in need, such as Asian groups

- Able to contribute, through partnerships, to the sustainability of the regeneration effort.

Below we give three case studies of Calderdale and Kirklees TEC, Batley City Challenge and Hackney Task Force that illustrate the use of some of these delivery mechanisms. We also include a case study of the use of the five roles as additional selection criteria in a major European funding programme.

Case study:
Batley Action (City Challenge)

As a case study, the strategy for area-based capacity building developed in Batley, West Yorkshire, especially demonstrates:

- The use of a variety of delivery mechanisms, including the fast tracking of selected organisations

- The conscious use of a systematic approach to area-based training needs analysis.

The area of Batley in Kirklees, West Yorkshire has suffered from high levels of unemployment and environmental neglect. A large proportion of the local population is Asian, and there are signs of multiple deprivation and an unemployment rate twice the national average. Batley City Challenge, now a limited company called Batley Action, was established in 1992, and the first year of its capacity building programme started in April 1993.

For this first year, the delivery mechanism was exclusively in the form of grant aid; a special fund of approximately £20,000 was established so that individuals and groups could define their own needs in terms of building capacity and training. While this system produced no shortage of high quality applications, the training requests being presented were not necessarily those which would enable Batley Action to deliver its forward strategy. Also, the level of organisational effectiveness within communities was less than anticipated. Batley Action therefore decided to take a more pro-active, approach which consisted of:

- Commissioning a systematic training needs analysis from CDF, identifying the training and development needs of individuals and groups active in the community and voluntary sector.

- Matching these against the needs of the regeneration programme to deliver the forward strategy

- Devising a clear set of recommendations with a Capacity Building Strategy arising from these.

The training needs analysis was carried out in the second half of 1994 and in early 1995 a new Capacity Building Strategy agreed on. The main features of this strategy were as follows:

Fast tracking
This would be a programme of intensive support and development work with a selected and limited number of community organisations. The selection criteria was that those organisations:

- Were in receipt of, or potentially in receipt of, major grant aid for community centre buildings, especially where these were to become community training venues.

- Were umbrella organisations that represented a wide cross-section of the local population

- Were representative of those sections of the community most in need, i e. Asian groups
- Could contribute through partnerships to the sustainability of the regeneration effort.

Baseline training

Capacity building included an ongoing and comprehensive provision of courses and seminars open to the community and voluntary sector on funding, organisational skills and management development. This is run in parallel to the fast tracking development work and is organised jointly with other local agencies such as the CVS.

Grant aid

An ongoing provision of grant aid is available for organisations and individuals who identify their own training needs or who are seeking more specialised training which can be cascaded into the community. This is an internally ring-fenced budget available exclusively for capacity building.

Another distinctive feature of Batley Action's capacity building activities is that they have consciously used the development of neighbourhood forums to act as a learning environment, where community representatives can increase their skill and experience in consultation and joint decision making.

For more information contact: Batley Action, telephone 01924 473456.

Case study
Calderdale and Kirklees TEC

This case study demonstrates a range of methods used by a TEC to support and develop capacity building.

Calderdale and Kirklees TEC is committed to working with the voluntary and community sector and recognises the vital role this sector plays in economic regeneration. The TEC has a track record of working with the black voluntary sector and recognises the importance of its role in promoting racial equality. The TEC believes it is of mutual benefit, particularly in relation to SRB and the expanding role of TECs in economic regeneration, to improve its own understanding of community development issues.

Recently, the TEC has been involved in a number of initiatives in particular to support black organisations in the area. This has taken a variety of forms, where they have:

- Helped to establish a black training network that could take on a developmental role and in turn assist as a channel of views on the needs of community organisations
- Funded a training needs survey of black organisations
- Funded a number of places for black community development workers on a community work training course
- Funded a consultancy support package for voluntary organisations, to develop their project applications to other funding sources such as ESF
- Funded two voluntary sector management training courses
- Allocated staff time to directly advise community groups on bids to other funding sources.

For more information contact: Calderdale and Kirklees TEC, telephone 01484 400770.

Case study
Hackney Task Force

This case study demonstrates an innovative three-part capacity building strategy.

In 1993/4 in liaison with other agencies, a three-year capacity building strategy was established with three main elements:

- The Community Training Programme was devised to help voluntary agencies develop their organisational and management skills, awarding participating organisations the 'Hackney quality standard'. This is a locally-designed set of measures of performance, concerning quality of management and service delivery (described in Part 2).

- The Community Mentoring Programme (described in Part 2).

- The establishment of a local training consortium. This involves staff and management committee members from seven refugee organisations based in the borough. These organisations in turn become a base for training, career guidance and business support for local unemployed refugees.

These three schemes, jointly funded by Hackney Task Force, Dalston City Partnership (City Challenge), Hackney Council and City and Inner London North Training and Enterprise Council, as well as other sources, involve expenditure of approximately £75,000 per year, and represent the majority of spending from these agencies on community-based capacity building. Some estate-based training programmes continue in parallel to the main programmes.

This three-part programme was designed in response to an initial review of both needs and provision.

- The community and voluntary sector were seen as unable to adequately respond to the growing demands of the contract culture and multi-source funding

- Existing provision of capacity building was seen as fragmented and not addressing these needs.

The policy issues that formed the underlying basis of the capacity building strategy were:

- The three schemes were initiated to respond to needs at a variety of levels; in particular the Community Training Programme would involve more established service delivery organisations while the mentoring scheme would prioritise newer and fledgling groups

- All three schemes focus on community enterprise and in particular a service delivery role; this was seen as the initial priority, with capacity building focusing on the potential partnership role, developed at a later stage, at least within the Task Force's regeneration initiatives

- The capacity building three-year programmes represent a co-ordinated inter-agency initiative to specifically address the formerly fragmented condition of capacity building activities. Because of the joint funding arrangement these schemes are borough-wide rather than limited to any specific regeneration programme area. The strategy also involves providing a database of information on resources and activities of the community and voluntary sector.

- All three schemes are resource-intensive and innovative, providing high quality support for a relatively limited number of organisations. The wider aim in addition to specific outputs related to any one scheme is to create an environment of enterprise culture in the borough where locally-based organisations will increasingly be equipped to respond to opportunities and take their own economic and community initiatives in future.

For more information contact: Hackney Task Force, telephone 0171-275 7100.

Case study
European Structural Funds in Yorkshire and Humberside

This case study demonstrates the innovative use of the five roles framework as the basis of additional selection criteria for a major funding programme.

In 1995/96 in Yorkshire and Humberside, the regional partnership adapted the five roles and their potential for community-based capacity building as additional selection criteria for the RECHAR Two and Objective Two programmes.

- In Yorkshire and Humberside, Objective Two Priority Six targeted a number of measures on key deprived areas within the region, both former coalfields and urban areas. The aim of Priority Six was to integrate members of such communities into the labour market and assist them in securing employment

- The RECHAR programme is targeted exclusively at former coalfield areas. Its measures include action to regenerate former mining communities and to create employment opportunities for their members.

During 1995 and 1996, the Yorkshire and Humberside regional partnership introduced additional selection criteria for both these major European programmes. This was presented as a scoring system for bids based on an adaptation of the five roles for the community in regeneration. The scoring is weighted, for example, giving a higher score to bids that indicate substantial levels of community participation. Bids also need to demonstrate how resources will be directed to capacity building activities in order to ensure effective community involvement and partnership.

Capacity building: scoring sheet
Indication of community involvement in Priority Six/RECHAR areas:

Community Benefit: 20 points
  1a Improves the quality of life
  1b Improves the prosperity of the area.

Community consultation: 10 points
  2a Reaches the maximum number of existing community groups
  2b Individual residents, minority and disadvantaged groups consulted
  2c Consultation extends its reach during the life of the project
  2d Create or enhance mechanisms for co-ordinating views of an
     increased proportion of the population, groups and organisations.

Community action: 10 points
  3a Ensures optimum conditions for community activity to flourish
  3b Targets set for enhancing the community sector
  3c Enhances the role and effectiveness of umbrella groups,
     support bodies and other community projects.

Community participation: 40 points
  4a The partnership includes community-based organisations
  4b Community-based organisations help to deliver the project
  4c Community groups and organisations will take on increased delivery roles
  4d Community economic initiatives supported by the project.

Community ownership: 20 points
  5a The project will be supported by the community in the long term
  5b Community organisations build up assets
  5c Part of a forward strategy to strengthen and sustain community participation.

Key issues concerning the application of this scoring system are:

- Within a total potential score of 100, each bid has to reach a minimum of 80 to proceed

- Within any one section each bid has to include plans for, or descriptions of, activities that demonstrate the majority but not necessarily all of the numbered points

- The scoring system is based on each section acting as a gate. If the content of any one section does not achieve the full score for that section, then the bid fails as it stands.

As can be seen, the five categories are adaptations of the roles presented earlier in the five roles framework. By introducing the gate system, the five roles have been developed into a hierarchical model of community involvement. The weighting pattern in particular acknowledges the importance of community involvement in delivery and partnership by giving a total of 40 points to that section.

An interesting feature of the RECHAR TWO programme is that one of the five measures is exclusively concerned with capacity building. For any one local partnership, these capacity building bids must be submitted prior to any others and act as the basis for all other project approvals.

This innovative and effective approach to the use of the five roles model in European Structural Funds could no doubt be adapted and built on in other regions.

For more information contact: Yorkshire and Humberside Government Office European Secretariat, telephone 0113 238211.

What is a Capacity Building Plan?

We now move on to look at the potential for capacity building plans. A community organisation may want to produce its own plan for the following reasons:

- It can help to ensure delivery of capacity building in their organisation is clearly targeted and well-organised

- It can help to obtain funding for the capacity building activities.

- Combined with others, it can contribute to the area-based strategy.

A plan for a community organisation could contain:

- A statement fn values and principles to underlie the delivery of capacity building, as discussed in Part 1

- A description of training and learning needs for individuals involved in the organisation, as discussed in Part 2

- An outline of present and future organisational development needs, as discussed in Part 3

- A description of the community organisation's own needs in terms of infrastructure, as described in Part 4

- A final section on costings as a summary of how capacity building for the organisation could be organised, funded and delivered, as described in this Part.

Evaluation also involves establishing an initial baseline position so that you can identify the progress made through the contribution of the capacity building activity.

This may read as rather a daunting list! However, it is useful to consider what a comprehensive plan could involve while accepting that in practice, time and energy may not allow this full version to be produced. Obviously, help may be required in assisting community organisations to produce their own plans; funding and regeneration bodies could consider this need as part of their grant-making criteria.

Here is an example of a capacity building plan based on the elements just described.

Bradwick Community Association capacity building plan

This plan covers the next two years of our work. The Bradwick Community Association is based in the Bradwick council estate, an area with high levels of unemployment and a lack of community facilities. As an association, following a recent consultation process, we plan to tackle these problems. Over the next two years the association intends to change into a development trust, to be better able to respond to these needs. We have recently been successful in obtaining SRB Challenge fund monies, to build a new community and enterprise centre and to employ three staff to run it. All these future activities are described in the Bradwick Community Association development plan, on which this capacity building plan is based.

This plan is divided into the following sections:

• People

• Organisation

• Infrastructure

• Principles.

We have written this plan because we now need financial help and other resources in order to provide capacity building activities over the next two years.

People

The Community Association already has among its members a range of useful skills and talents. However, looking ahead there are many challenges and changes in the pipeline that will require new areas of knowledge and skill:

• Establishing a new structure (development trust)

• Organising construction of the new building

• Recruiting and managing new staff

• Running the community centre and enterprise centre

• Generally relating to new council officers, the TEC and local businesses.

We have carried out a review of our training needs, using the help of the training officer from the CVS. From this we have a planned programme of training, assuming the building will be up and running in a year's time. In this programme, one session is approximately three hours.

Year One

- Eight sessions: management skills – recruitment and selection; managing staff; running a building
- Two sessions: development trusts – constitution, finance
- Four sessions: confidence building – assertion training
- Mentoring scheme: two committee members to obtain support from two staff at a neighbouring development trust
- Placement: one committee member to go on a weekly half-day placement at a graphic design and printing studio
- Exchange visits: to two multi-purpose community centres.

Year Two

- Eight Sessions: management and communication skills – publicity; teamwork; communication with neighbourhood and with local organisations
- Four sessions: finance and planning skills
- Two Sessions: understanding partnerships
- Placement: financial adviser from a local company invited to join the trust board
- Visits: no definite plans yet.

We are currently exploring how many of these courses can be accredited and lead to useful qualifications for the participants.

The organisation

We recently employed a consultant for three days, to help us look at our future needs when an organisation such as the Association changes over the next two years. From this review the following key areas of support will be needed:

Year One

- Legal advice on the constitution of the development trust
- Business advice on how to manage workspace in the new enterprise centre
- Facilitation work to help establish sub-committees within the trust to manage the two centres
- A six-monthly 'awayday' review of progress
- Team building sessions with new partners to the development trust
- Workshops on anti-racism to help us develop a fuller equal opportunities policy
- Advice and practical help in applying for European funds.

Year Two

- A community consultation exercise to keep in touch with our neighbourhood

- A six-monthly 'away day' review
- Ten support/supervision sessions for the staff team
- Advice and help with setting up a cafe/bar as a separate company
- An outside evaluation of two years' work.

Community infrastructure

In planning our activities both for the next few months and over the next two years, we have reviewed our wider needs for resources and information as follows:

- Immediate access is needed to cheap printing facilities to print, for example, a newsletter and meetings leaflets
- Funding to allow us to employ a consultant for 30 days over the next two years
- Access to a business adviser as outlined
- Help from a community worker over the next two years at an approximate rate of one day per week.
- Funding for a computer with Internet access to encourage information exchange with other community organisations in the city
- Use on four occasions over the next year of a venue for presentation to the TEC and businesses
- Use of a suitable venue for the two 'awaydays'.
- We would also like to request a training course for staff in the authority's Economic Development Unit on how to relate to the community.

Principles

We believe our capacity building plan should be based on the following principles:

- The starting point is the existing valuable resource of skills, knowledge and talents that volunteers, members and friends of the Association already have; our capacity building activities will build from those strengths to make all of us even more effective in our work
- We recognise and welcome the contribution of people in our association and neighbourhood from a variety of cultural backgrounds. We hope the capacity building activities reflect this diversity and we appreciate feedback to ensure it does
- We will work to ensure our capacity building activities are open to all sections of the community. We hope this will include, for example, fully accessible rooms for training and meetings and crèche facilities available on request
- We invite other local organisations to join us in sharing skills, ideas and approaches; we are especially keen to find out about community- run enterprise centres
- We do not see capacity building as only to do with 'the community'. We invite 'professionals' and staff in the council and other agencies working in our area to look at their own capacity building needs. We need to develop a joint way of working so that we can understand each other

- Finall,y we request that organisations such as national voluntary organisations, the council and the TEC recognise that as members of our community association and neighbourhood we have a lot to offer – knowledge of the area and its problems and above all, since we live here, a commitment to improvement and change.

Key points

This example of a capacity building plan has been intentionally written to demonstrate points discussed earlier in Parts 1, 2, 3 and 4. Normally, a plan would also include notes on costings. It is included as a full version of how a capacity building plan could be presented while accepting that in practice, it would be demanding for any community organisation to have developed its plan this far. However it acts as a checklist that can be adapted to the needs and resources of any individual group or organisation. Key points about this plan are:

- Planning for capacity building over a two-year time period is not easy. The second year activities in such a plan may have less detail than the first year, but this can be revised nearer the time. When devising a plan it is important not to alienate group members by planning in great detail too far ahead. In the example given, to have got as far as devising a capacity building plan required some outside help from a training officer and a specialist.

- The capacity building plan refers to and is based on the larger Community Association's development plan. This latter plan is a more conventional action plan, describing the aims and objectives for the group's activities over the next year or beyond. Ideally, this is devised first and a capacity building plan grows from it. In reality this may not always be possible or even desirable; it may be that for a temporary period a community organisation needs a high level of support and capacity building, to reach the stage where it can consider its own action plan.

- It is useful to include a statement on underlying principles. Obviously, each community organisation can devise and decide on its own set of 'principles'; the list offered here contains beliefs held by many successful community groups. However, whatever form it takes, it is useful to include some statement on principles or values in a plan, because otherwise these may get lost in practical arrangements on funding and delivery. It may be useful to include in a capacity building plan definitions of key concepts offered at various points in this resource book, such as capacity building, training and organisational development. These can help to clarify what the plan is aiming to do, and avoid unnecessary misunderstandings.

Devising a Capacity Building Plan

In this section we explore the work involved in actually devising and compiling a Capacity Building Plan. This could involve a number of events or stages:

- Discussion and exploration as to why one is needed and what it could involve; this would include reviewing needs arising from the community group's Development Plan if one already exists
- An open consultation meeting with all members of the committee, group, association, trust board, neighbourhood, network etc. as appropriate
- Workshop sessions exploring training needs and organisational development needs, as described in Parts 2 and 3
- Workshop sessions reviewing wider infrastructure needs as described in Part 4, perhaps involving representatives from the council, TEC, and other community organisations
- Writing a draft Capacity Building Plan which is circulated for consultation and comments
- Completion of the final version.

Three underlying themes, referred to in Part 1, are useful to guide the work involved in the process of devising such a plan:

- The plan should have a *comprehensive* look at capacity building needs. 'Comprehensive' means based on an examination of training needs, organisational needs and infrastructure needs. Many groups only look at training needs and miss out any consideration of the other areas
- The plan should have a *systematic* approach to assessing needs. In the past many community organisations have been involved in training, but often in an *ad hoc* manner. Members go on a course or to a workshop because it 'looks interesting'. As described in Part 2, there are methods available to help community groups to identify training needs which can be used – with flexibility – with the same degree of precision as that achieved in large organisations. Equally, there are methods available to clarify organisational needs and some aspects of infrastructure needs
- The plan considers existing needs but is also *forward looking*. Again, a limitation on much past practice in terms of support to community organisations is that is does not adequately help the group to look ahead to changes in the pipeline that will require new structures and systems. An approach based on 'cross that bridge when we come to it' is not realistic nowadays, given the increasingly complex demands placed on the voluntary and community sector. Planning ahead and understanding the implications of changes yet to come is difficult; and when encouraging groups to adopt this approach, it is also important to go at a pace that does not alienate or lose less confident members.

Using a Capacity Building Plan

The plan, once completed, can be used in at least the following three ways:

- *As a focus for involving people in the community organisation.* Training, visits and 'away days' are all very tangible events around which to invite and involve new and existing members. Successful visits, 'away days' and training events can also act as useful team building exercises in their own right – without ever needing to call them that! Having a plan which lists future activities is one way of attracting and involving new members.

- *As a means to gaining additional funding.* Although based around the needs of the community organisation, many TECs will consider funding a well-prepared capacity building plan as a potential way of addressing some of the needs of the local labour market, through increasing the 'transferable skills' of the 'non-traditional learner'. Equally, a capacity building plan can form part of an SRB Challenge Fund or European Funds Objective Two application. In fact, as discussed earlier, some SRB bids have been exclusively based around a capacity building district or city-wide programme.

- *As a contribution to an area-based strategy.* A capacity building plan can carry considerable weight as a negotiating and campaigning tool in encouraging regeneration agencies to look properly at the issues of local management and locally-based long-term involvement. Ideally several community organisations in one area would develop capacity building plans at roughly the same time so these could forcefully feed in a grassroots perspective to the strategic overview developed by a regeneration agency.

The evaluation of capacity building

In this section we begin to explore the issues involved in the evaluation of capacity building, in the context of regeneration. This can involve evaluation at two levels:

- At the level of the community organisation as the main participant in the capacity building activities

- At the level of the regeneration agency as the main funder of capacity building activities.

There is also a need to identify the difference between what is essentially a process of monitoring – that is, collecting usually factual information concerning outputs – and evaluation, which is a more thorough process of assessing effectiveness against stated objectives. We now explore both the community organisation and regeneration agency levels, with discussion on the difference between evaluation and monitoring.

Evaluations at community organisation level

This could involve the evaluation of the various forms of training described in Part 2 and the effectiveness of short term assistance described in Part 3. The evaluation of capacity building activities is worth carrying out, because it:

- Helps to improve the process next time

- Helps to ensure future focus on priorities

- Helps indicate if the activity should be changed

- Demonstrates to funders resources are being carefully used

- Helps the specialists and trainers to improve their practice

- Affirms the lessons learned to group members.

We give here a brief introduction, using the headings of how, when, and what; for further information, publications on evaluation are listed below.

How

Evaluation is a process of collecting information to measure effectiveness on the basis of agreed criteria. The collection of information – often called monitoring – usually involves collecting 'hard' and 'soft' information:

- Hard information – facts and figures ie. quantitative
- Soft information – perceptions, views, attitudes, ie. qualitative.

Both forms of information can be collected through a variety of methods for example, discussion, interviews, questionnaires, observation and feedback sessions, and from both internal and external sources. Hard information is often the basis of measuring outputs, however an over-emphasis on this aspect alone is a very limited form of assessing effectiveness. Overall effectiveness can only be measured if there is a clear statement at the start of the capacity building work, as to:

- What are you trying to achieve in the capacity building activity?
- How will you know you have achieved it?

The main aspect to evaluate is real changes in practice – not just how well written the evaluation report is!

This involves stating clear objectives, including specific targets that will indicate achievement, and agreeing on how both hard and soft information is to be collected during and after the work. Remember though, you may also achieve some useful things you did not set out to achieve! Other useful general questions to consider in an evaluation are:

- Are there unexpected positive outcomes?
- Are there unexpected negative outcomes?
- If the goals were not achieved why is this?
- What useful learning has there been generally about the process of using trainers, mentors, secondees or specialists?
- What new training or organisational development needs does the group now have?

When

- *At the beginning.* At the start of the activity objectives need to be clearly set and a baseline position established that you can later measure against
- *At a mid-way point.* This can be a review session held for example at a mid-way point, in the specialist's, secondee's, mentor's or trainer's involvement. For longer term projects involving capacity building, this could be an annual review
- *At the end of the work.* This can be a session held near the end of the specialist's, secondee's, mentor's or trainer's involvement. Equally, it could happen at the end of a visit or placement
- *Some time after completion.* This could be a month, three months or more after completion of the work, and look more at changes in individual practice and in the organisation.

As indicated, a key to effective evaluation is establishing an initial baseline position so that you can identify the progress made through the contribution of the capacity building activity. Consequently the evaluation needs to be planned for and considered before the start of the capacity building activity and ideally, an assessment of the baseline position be made prior to the start of any capacity building programmes.

What

The evaluation can cover four main issues:

- How effective was the specialist or trainer? For example did they deliver the training course well?

- Did the work achieve its aim? For example did the participants learn the required skills?

- Did the work achieve the aim with efficient use of resources? That is, was it cost effective?

- Did achieving the aim led to any real changes in the organisation? For example were the new skills were used to help the group be more effective?

With these main questions there are three problems to consider, here is a training-based example:

- The trainer may have been very effective in delivering the course but, due to unforeseen circumstances, the aim of the work was not achieved. The training course content, for example, may have unearthed huge tensions in the group that needed dealing with at their request, leaving less time for group members to acquire new skills

- Alternatively, the aim of the trainer's work with the group may have been achieved, but the skills were not then used by group members. There may be other blocks to the use of skills that have not been addressed

- Finally, there is the case where the skills are used but the reason for the group's increased efficiency is due to other factors – such as new members joining.

In other words, forces in the group or in the group's environment can complicate judging the effectiveness of the role of the specialist or trainer. This type of problem is common to many forms of social research. Rather than let it become a block, there is a need to evaluate capacity building in a conscious manner, while recognising that a number of different factors may be present in any outcome. A useful approach is to distinguish between information, that is what happened, and the actual interpretation of the information, that is why it happened.

Some key points in general on evaluation are:

- Have consultation and discussion on it at an early stage in the group so members are open to participating in the evaluation as appropriate and do not feel threatened by it

- Don't be too ambitious – remember thorough evaluation of capacity building programmes can need specialist assistance in its own right.
- Work out which parts of the capacity building activity are the most important ones to evaluate.

Evaluation at regeneration agency level

Here the agency will be concerned about the effectiveness of capacity building on an area basis and in relation to the aims and objectives of the overall regeneration programme. Large and diverse capacity building programmes can be evaluated by first breaking them down into identifiable schemes, with particular objectives in each case and then making an overall assessment. The system of evaluation described so far will be useful in any discrete capacity building scheme. Key issues in this process are:

- *Evaluation is not just monitoring.* The establishment of output targets should not be confused with the more thorough process of evaluation. Output targets are usually presented in terms of hard information, such as numbers of participants or numbers of groups assisted with organisational development and so on. Indicators are needed that can cater for and reflect the quality of the experience and the outcomes arising from the outputs. In particular, indicators are needed that address the less-tangible process aspects of capacity building, for example those linked to the underlying principles of empowerment. CDF is currently carrying out a major research project to identify indicators to measure community development outputs and outcomes which include capacity building indicators.

For more information contact: the Scottish Centre for Community Development, telephone 0141 248 1924.

- *Capacity building is a distinct area of activity.* The evaluation of capacity building should not be confused with and dominated by the evaluation of the regeneration programme itself. Unless the regeneration programme is exclusively concerned with capacity building – as has happened in some cases – there will be a need to identify the specific aspects of spending related to capacity building. Obviously there will be some overlap but the point is that this overlap needs to be made explicit, so that the particular activities focusing on capacity building can be evaluated.

For examples of targets on capacity building established within the five roles framework for the wider aims of regeneration programmes, see Regeneration and the Community *(CDF 1996).*

- *Efficiency needs to be evaluated as well as effectiveness.* The evaluation needs to focus on issues of value for money, efficiency as well as effectiveness. For example, a community mentoring scheme may have been very effective in enhancing the managerial skills of five organisations in the regeneration area; however a comparison of costs reveals that it was a resource-intensive way to achieve this, compared to for example a course-based training programme.

For a useful examination of these issues see A Framework For the Evaluation of Regeneration Projects and Programmes *(HM Treasury 1995).*

- *Equality issues need to be evaluated as well as efficiency and effectiveness.* The aim of the capacity building project may be to specifically involve marginalised groups; its level of success in achieving this goal would consequently need to be assessed. Even without such specific aims, as argued in this publication, the principle of equality should underlie the provision of capacity building in all aspects of its organisation.

For an informed exploration of these issues see Evaluating Social Development Projects *(Marsden and Oakley 1990).*

- *The effectiveness of the community infrastructure should be included.* The evaluation will need to identify the effectiveness of community infrastructure as the environment within which community organisations operate. If an audit of resource needs, as described in Part 4 has been carried out at an initial point in the regeneration programme, it can be used as a baseline point to compare progress achieved by a later date. Equally the effectiveness of community development support can be evaluated through use of a system of proposed outcomes.

For information on outcomes of community work see Strong Communities, Effective Government: The Role of Community Work *(Barr et al 1995)*

- *Evaluation at area level may require a pluralist approach.* As already suggested, the regeneration agency will be concerned about the effectiveness of capacity building on an area basis and in relation to the aims and objectives of the overall regeneration programme. There will obviously be a relationship between the concerns of community organisations in participating in capacity building that meets their needs and the concerns of the agency in delivering an effective and sustainable regeneration programme. A useful way forward is to adopt a pluralistic approach to the evaluation, accepting that a range of objectives exist, shared to varying degrees by different parties. However, given the definition of capacity building included in the introduction, we would argue that evaluation should be based on a key target of increasing the effectiveness of community groups, in terms such as the group's own estimate of whether it is achieving its goals.

For an informative discussion of the pluralistic approach to evaluation, see The Evaluation of Training in the Social Services *(Bramley and Pahl 1996).*

Some general points concerning evaluation at both community organisation and agency level include:

- Build time and resources for evaluation into the brief and funding for the work. The scale of the evaluation should broadly match the size and significance of the capacity building project
- Evaluation and monitoring is best established on a regular basis so that systems can be set up to cater for information collection, and organisations can get used to a regular pattern of reviewing progress

- Evaluations can be based on comparisons between similar projects, comparing levels of effectiveness for broadly similar work, while recognising that differences may be due to external factors
- The information collecting process can in many cases be an opportunity for community involvement
- Evaluation methods should allow opportunities to learn from and contribute to good practice established in other regeneration programmes
- As indicated above, the evaluation process may itself indicate new learning needs for groups and organisations. In this way the evaluation process can be a useful aid to effective planning, based on a cycle of: needs are identified; capacity building activities are organised and run; an evaluation is carried out; new needs are identified.

This section on evaluation at area level has not attempted to systematically examine the nature of meaningful outputs and outcomes in capacity building, a complex subject which needs a resource book in its own right! Some of the issues have been raised with reference to sources for further information and guidance.

Further reading

Ball, M. (1988) *Evaluation in the Voluntary Sector*, The Forbes Trust.

Barr, A. Drysdale, J. Purcell, R. and Ross, C. (1995) *Strong Communities, Effective Government: The Role of Community Work*, Scottish Community Development Centre.

Bramley and Pahl (1996) *The Evaluation of Training in the Social Services*, National Institute for Social Work.

CDF (1996) *Regeneration and the Community*.

Chanan,G., Dale, P., Humm, J., (1996) *Community Involvement in Two Areas of Sandwell; Final report of a Baseline Study of Tipton and Hateley Heath*, unpublished, CDF.

HM Treasury (1995) *A Framework For the Evaluation of Regeneration Projects and Programmes*, Housing and Policy Team.

Health Promotion Wales (1996) *The Mentoring and Evaluation Scheme Action Booklet*

Marsden, D. and Oakley, P. (1990) *Evaluating Social Development Projects*, Oxfam.

Skinner, S. (1992) *Training and how not to panic*, CETU.

Skinner, S. (1995) *Directories and Resource Guides: How to produce them*, CDF.

(1996) *Socal and Economic Inclusion through Regional Development* Office for Official Publications of the European Communities.

Concluding Remarks

Capacity building plans at community group level are essential building blocks for the long term sustainability of the regeneration initiative. In parallel to this, the regeneration agency needs to plan ahead for its own ultimate withdrawal from the area, developing structures and systems that will lead to a lasting impact:

'Capacity building is about making and sustaining change. It involves enabling an individual or an organisation to do something more than they could do before. It also involves building their ability to sustain that improvement without the support provided by the capacity building initiative'

Bethnal Green City Challenge capacity building strategy

'Effective capacity building will increase the strength and independence of the community sector that may increasingly set the agenda in terms of regeneration.'
Community work manager

Through the use of the Five Roles Framework and a range of delivery mechanisms, regeneration agencies have the potential to organise and direct resources towards specific outcomes in the development of the community and voluntary sector in the regeneration area. However as argued earlier, to be effective this planning activity needs to be based on an assessment of training and organisational needs. It also requires a review of infrastructure needs, as well as a process of community consultation. Only if organised and carried out consistently based on the underlying principles of equality and empowerment will the community achieve any sense of ownership and involvement; as discussed in Part 1, these features are essential elements in the sustainability of the regeneration programme.

Also essential is recognition by the regeneration agency and other major organisations active in the area on the need for a programme of professional capacity building. True partnership working is about an acceptance on both sides of the table that a process of relationship building, and learning about effective communication, is necessary.

'We have no exit strategy – we live here!'
Community leader

This process, on the part of professionals based in large organisations and regeneration agencies, will itself help to create a more informed understanding about the wealth of skills, experience and knowledge that already exists at grassroots community level. This wealth is the basis of building community strengths.

Feedback Form

If you'd like to help us develop our publications to be more effective for community development, please photocopy this questionnaire and fill it in, or write us a letter, sending or faxing it to us at:

CDF Publications
60 Highbury Grove
London N5 2AG Tel: 0171 226 5375; Fax: 0171 704 0313

Please complete and return to the address above

What I like most about this pack is:

What I like least about this pack is:

What I found most useful about this pack is:

What I found least useful about this pack is:

This pack helped my work develop by:

In the space below, or in a separate letter, please let us know any other comments you would like to make or any ideas for future publications. We welcome your suggestions.

YOUR NAME

ORGANISATION

ADDRESS

DATE   **TELEPHONE**